MW01026460

THE JEWISH PEOPLE
AND THEIR
SACRED SCRIPTURES
IN THE
CHRISTIAN BIBLE

THE JEWISH PEOPLE AND THEIR SACRED SCRIPTURES IN THE CHRISTIAN BIBLE

Pontifical Biblical Commission

Pauline BOOKS & MEDIA BOSTON

All rights reserved. No part of this book may be reproduced or transmitted in any form or by any means, electronic or mechanical, including photocopying, recording or by any information storage and retrieval system, without permission in writing from the publisher.

Vatican Translation

ISBN 0-8198-3975-2

Copyright © 2002, Libreria Editrice Vaticana

Printed and published in the U.S.A. by Pauline Books & Media, 50 Saint Pauls Avenue, Boston MA 02130-3491.

www.pauline.org

Pauline Books & Media is the publishing house of the Daughters of St. Paul, an international congregation of women religious serving the Church with the communications media.

1 2 3 4 5 6 7 8 9   07 06 05 04 03 02

Contents

PREFACE

The internal unity of the Church's Bible, which comprises the Old and New Testaments, was a central theme in the theology of the Church Fathers. That it was far from being a theoretical problem only is evident from dipping, so to speak, into the spiritual journey of one of the greatest teachers of Christendom, St. Augustine of Hippo. In 373, the nineteen-year-old Augustine already had his first decisive experience of conversion. His reading of one of the works of Cicero—*Hortensius,* since lost—brought about a profound transformation which he himself described later on as follows: "Toward you, O Lord, it directed my prayers.... I began to pick myself up to return to you…. How ardent I was, O my God, to let go of the earthly and take wings back to you" (*Confessions,* III, 4, 81). For the young African who, as a child, had received the salt that made him a catechumen, it was clear that conversion to God entailed attachment to Christ; apart from Christ, he could not truly find God. So he went from Cicero to the Bible and experienced a terrible disappointment: in the exacting legal prescriptions of the Old Testament, in its complex and at times brutal narratives, he failed to find that Wisdom toward which he wanted to travel. In the course of his search, he encountered certain people who proclaimed a new spiritual Christianity, one which understood the Old Testament as spiritually deficient and repugnant; a Christianity in which Christ had no need of the witness of the Hebrew prophets. Those people promised him a Christianity of pure and simple reason, a Christianity in which Christ was the great illuminator, leading human beings to true self-knowledge. These were the Manicheans.[1]

The great promise of the Manicheans proved illusory, but the problem remained unresolved for all that. Augustine was unable to convert to the Christianity of the Catholic Church until he had learned, through Ambrose, an interpretation of the Old Testament that made transparent the relationship of Israel's Bible to Christ, and thus revealed that Wisdom for which he searched. What was overcome was not only the exterior obstacle of an unsatisfactory literary form of the Old Latin Bible, but above all the interior obstacle of a book that was no longer just a document of the religious history of a particular people, with all its strayings and mistakes. It revealed instead a Wisdom addressed to all and came from God. Through the transparency of Israel's long, slow historical journey, that reading of Israel's Bible identified Christ, the Word, eternal Wisdom. It was, therefore, of fundamental importance not only for Augustine's decision of faith; it was and is the basis for the faith decision of the Church as a whole.

---

1. See the presentation of this phase of Augustine's spiritual journey in the work of PETER BROWN, *Augustine of Hippo, A Biography* (London: Faber & Faber, 1967, 40 – 45).

But is all this true? Is it also demonstrable and tenable still today? From the viewpoint of historical-critical exegesis, it seems—at first glance, in any case—that exactly the opposite is true. It was in 1920 that the well-known liberal theologian Adolf Harnack formulated the following thesis: "The rejection of the Old Testament in the second century [an allusion to Marcion] was an error which the great Church was right in resisting; holding on to it in the 16th century was a disaster from which the Reformation has not yet been able to extricate itself; but to maintain it since the 19th century in Protestantism as a canonical document equal in value to the New Testament, that is the result of religious and ecclesial paralysis."[2]

Is Harnack right? At first glance several things seem to point in that direction. The exegetical method of Ambrose did indeed open the way to the Church for Augustine, and in its basic orientation—allowing, of course, for a considerable measure of variance in the details—became the foundation of Augustine's faith in the biblical Word of God, consisting of two parts, and nevertheless composing a unity. But it is still possible to make the following objection: Ambrose had learned this exegesis from the school of Origen, who had been the first to develop its methodology. But Origen, it may be said, only applied to the Bible the allegorical method of interpretation which was practiced in the Greek world, to explain the religious texts of antiquity—in particular, Homer—and not only produced a hellenization intrinsically foreign to the

2. A. von Harnack, *Marcion,* 1920. Reissued Darmstadt 1985, XII and 217.

biblical word, but used a method that was unreliable, because, in the last analysis, it tried to preserve as something sacred what was, in fact, only a witness to a moribund culture. Yet, it is not that simple. Much more than the Greek exegesis of Homer, Origen could build on the Old Testament interpretation which was born in a Jewish milieu, especially in Alexandria, beginning with Philo who sought in a totally appropriate way to introduce the Bible to Greeks who were long in search of the one biblical God beyond polytheism. And Origen had studied at the feet of the rabbis. He eventually developed specifically Christian principles: the internal unity of the Bible as a rule of interpretation, Christ as the meeting point of all the Old Testament pathways.[3]

In whatever way one judges the detailed exegesis of Origen and Ambrose, its deepest basis was neither Hellenistic allegory, nor Philo nor rabbinic methods. Strictly speaking—leaving aside the details of interpretation—its basis was the New Testament itself. Jesus of Nazareth claimed to be the true heir to the Old Testament—"the Scriptures"—and to offer a true interpretation, which, admittedly, was not that of

---

3. The decisive breakthrough for an appreciation of Origen's exegesis was made by H. DE LUBAC in his work *Histoire et Esprit. L'intelligence de l'Écriture d'après Origène* (Paris, 1950). Since then, the works of H. CROUZEL especially merit attention (for example, *Origene,* 1985). A good overview of the state of research is given by H. J. SIEBEN in his *Einleitung zu Origenes.* In Lucam homiliae, Fribourg, 1991, pp. 7–53. A synthesis of the various works of H. DE LUBAC on the question of the interpretation of Scripture is given in the work edited by J. VODERHOLZER, *H. de Lubac, Typologie, Allegorese, Geistiger Sinn.* Studien zur Geschichte der christlichen Schriftauslegung, Johannes Verlag, Fribourg, 1999.

the schools, but came from the authority of the Author himself: "He taught them as one having authority, and not as the scribes" (Mk 1:22). The Emmaus narrative also expresses this claim: "Beginning with Moses and all the prophets, he interpreted to them the things about himself in all the Scriptures" (Lk 24:27). The New Testament authors sought to ground this claim concretely, in particular Matthew, but Paul as well, by using rabbinic methods of interpretation to show that the scribal interpretation led to Christ as the key to the "Scriptures." For the authors and founders of the New Testament, the Old Testament was simply "the Scriptures": it was only later that the developing Church gradually formed a New Testament canon which was also Sacred Scripture, but in the sense that it still presupposed Israel's Bible to be such, the Bible read by the apostles and their disciples, and now called the Old Testament, which provided the interpretative key.

From this viewpoint, the Fathers of the Church created nothing new when they gave a Christological interpretation to the Old Testament; they only developed and systematized what they themselves had already discovered in the New Testament. This fundamental synthesis for the Christian faith would become problematic when historical consciousness developed rules of interpretation that made Patristic exegesis appear nonhistorical and so objectively indefensible. In the context of humanism, with its newfound historical awareness, but especially in the context of his doctrine of justification, Luther invented a new formula relating the two parts of the Christian Bible, one no longer based on the internal harmony of the Old and New Testaments, but on their essential dialectic linkage within an existential history of salvation, the antithesis between Law and Gospel. Bultmann modernized this approach when he said that the Old Testament is fulfilled in Christ by foundering. More radical is the proposition of Harnack mentioned above; as far as I can see, it was not generally accepted, but it was completely logical for an exegesis for which texts from the past could have no meaning other than that intended by the authors in their historical context. That the biblical authors in the centuries before Christ, writing in the Old Testament, intended to refer in advance to Christ and New Testament faith, looks to the modern historical consciousness as highly unlikely.

As a result, the triumph of historical-critical exegesis seemed to sound the death knell for the Christian interpretation of the Old Testament initiated by the New Testament itself. It is not a question here of historical details, as we have seen; it is the very foundations of Christianity that are being questioned. It is understandable then that nobody has since embraced Harnack's position and made the definitive break with the Old Testament that Marcion prematurely wished to accomplish. What would have remained, our New Testament, would itself be devoid of meaning. The document of the Pontifical Biblical Commission introduced by this Preface declares: "Without the Old Testament, the New Testament would be an incomprehensible book, a plant deprived of its roots and destined to dry up and wither" (n. 84).

From this perspective, one can appreciate the enormous task the Pontifical Biblical Commission set for itself in deciding to tackle the theme of the relationship between the Old and New Testaments. If the impasse presented by Harnack is to be overcome, the very concept of an interpretation of his-

16

torical texts must be broadened and deepened enough to be tenable in today's liberal climate, and capable of application, especially to biblical texts received in faith as the Word of God. Important contributions have been made in this direction over recent decades. The Pontifical Biblical Commission made its own contribution in the document published in 1993 on *The Interpretation of the Bible in the Church.* The recognition of the multidimensional nature of human language, not staying fixed to a particular moment in history, but having a hold on the future, is an aid that permits a greater understanding of how the Word of God can avail of the human word to confer on a history in progress a meaning that surpasses the present moment and yet brings out, precisely in this way, the unity of the whole. Beginning from that document, and mindful of methodology, the Biblical Commission examined the relationship between the many great thematic threads of both Testaments, and was able to conclude that the Christian hermeneutic of the Old Testament, admittedly very different from that of Judaism, "corresponds nevertheless to a potentiality of meaning that is really present in the texts" (n. 64). This is a conclusion which seems to me to be of great importance for the pursuit of dialogue, but above all, for grounding the Christian faith.

In its work the Biblical Commission could not ignore the contemporary context, where the shock of the Shoah has put the whole question under a new light. Two main problems are posed: can Christians, after all that has happened, still claim in good conscience to be the legitimate heirs of Israel's Bible? Have they the right to propose a Christian interpretation of this Bible, or should they not instead, respectfully and humbly, renounce any claim that, in light of what has happened, must look like a usurpation? The second question follows from the first: in its presentation of the Jews and the Jewish people, has not the New Testament itself contributed to creating a hostility toward the Jewish people that provided a support for the ideology of those who wished to destroy Israel? The Commission set about addressing those two questions. It is clear that a Christian rejection of the Old Testament would not only put an end to Christianity itself as indicated above, but in addition would prevent the fostering of positive relations between Christians and Jews, precisely because they would lack common ground. In light of what has happened, what ought to emerge now is a new respect for the Jewish interpretation of the Old Testament. On this subject, the document says two things. First it declares that "the Jewish reading of the Bible is a possible one, in continuity with the Jewish Sacred Scriptures from the Second Temple period, a reading analogous to the Christian reading which developed in parallel fashion" (n. 22). It adds that Christians can learn a great deal from a Jewish exegesis practiced for more than 2,000 years; in return, Christians may hope that Jews can profit from Christian exegetical research (n. 22). I think this analysis will prove useful for the pursuit of Judeo-Christian dialogue, as well as for the interior formation of Christian consciousness.

The question of how Jews are presented in the New Testament is dealt with in the second part of the document; the "anti-Jewish" texts there are methodically analyzed for an understanding of them. Here, I want only to underline an aspect which seems to me to be particularly important. The document shows that the reproofs addressed to Jews in the

New Testament are neither more frequent nor more virulent than the accusations against Israel in the Law and the Prophets, at the heart of the Old Testament itself (n. 87). They belong to the prophetic language of the Old Testament and are, therefore, to be interpreted in the same way as the prophetic messages: they warn against contemporary aberrations, but they are essentially of a temporary nature and always open to new possibilities of salvation.

To the members of the Biblical Commission, I wish to express gratitude and appreciation for their work. From their discussions, patiently pursued over several years, this document has emerged which, I am convinced, can offer a precious aid to the study of one of the central questions of the Christian faith, as well as to the search so important for a new understanding between Christians and Jews.

Rome, the feast of the Ascension, 2001
+ JOSEPH Cardinal RATZINGER

Introduction[4]

1. Modern times have made Christians more aware of the close fraternal bonds that unite them to the Jewish people. During the Second World War (1939–1945), tragic events, or more precisely, abominable crimes subjected the Jewish people to a terrible ordeal that threatened their very existence throughout most of Europe. In those circumstances, some Christians failed to exhibit the spiritual resistance to be expected from disciples of Christ, and did not take the appropriate initiatives to counter them. Other Christians, though, did generously aid Jews in danger, often at the risk of their own lives. In the wake of such an enormous tragedy, Christians are faced with the need to reassess their relations with the Jewish people. Already considerable research and reflection have been done in this direction. The Pontifical Biblical Commission, insofar as it is competent, wishes to participate in this endeavor. Since this obviously does not include addressing all the historical and contemporary aspects of the problem, the Commission confines itself to the current state of research in the field of biblical exegesis.

---

4. Translated from the French by Maurice Hogan.

The question which is asked is the following: what relations does the Christian Bible establish between Christians and the Jewish people? The general answer is clear: between Christians and Jews, the Christian Bible establishes many close relations. Firstly, because the Christian Bible is composed, for the greater part, of the "Holy Scriptures" (Rm 1:2) of the Jewish people, which Christians call the "Old Testament"; secondly, because the Christian Bible is also comprised of a collection of writings which, while expressing faith in Christ Jesus, puts them in close relationship with the Jewish Sacred Scriptures. This second collection, as we know, is called the "New Testament," an expression correlative to "Old Testament."

That an intimate relationship exists between them is undeniable. A closer examination, however, reveals that this is not a straightforward relationship, but a very complex one that ranges from perfect accord on some points to one of great tension on others. A careful study is therefore necessary. The Biblical Commission has devoted the past few years to this study. The results, which make no claim of being exhaustive, are presented here in three chapters. The first chapter lays the foundations by demonstrating that the New Testament recognizes the authority of the Old Testament as divine revelation, and that the New Testament cannot be properly understood apart from the Old Testament and the Jewish tradition which transmits it. The second chapter then examines analytically how the writings of the New Testament appropriate the rich content of the Old Testament by developing its basic themes in the light of Jesus Christ. Finally, the third chapter reviews the various attitudes which the New Testament writings express regarding the Jews, following, in this respect, the example of the Old Testament itself.

In this way the Biblical Commission hopes to advance the dialogue between Christians and Jews with clarity and in a spirit of mutual esteem and affection.

I

The Sacred Scriptures of the Jewish People Are a Fundamental Part of the Christian Bible

2. It is above all by virtue of its historical origin that the Christian community discovers its links with the Jewish people. Indeed, the person in whom it puts its faith, Jesus of Nazareth, is himself a son of this people. So too are the Twelve whom he chose "to be with him and to be sent out to proclaim the message" (Mk 3:14). In the beginning, the apostolic preaching was addressed only to the Jews and proselytes, pagans associated with the Jewish community (cf. Acts 2:11). Christianity, then, came to birth in the bosom of first century Judaism. Although it gradually detached itself from Judaism, the Church could never forget its Jewish roots, something clearly attested in the New Testament; it even recognized a certain priority for Jews, for the Gospel is the "power of God for salvation to everyone who has faith, *to the Jew first* and also to the Greek" (Rm 1:16).

A perennial manifestation of this link to their beginnings is the acceptance by Christians of the Sacred Scriptures of the Jewish people as the Word of God addressed to themselves as well. Indeed, the Church has accepted as inspired by God all the writings contained in the Hebrew Bible as well as those in the Greek Bible. The title "Old Testament" given to this collection of writings is an expression coined by the Apostle Paul to designate the writings attributed to Moses (cf. 2 Co 3:14–15). Its scope has been extended, since the end of the second century, to include other Jewish writings in Hebrew, Aramaic, and Greek. The title "New Testament" takes its origin from a message in the Book of Jeremiah which announced a "new covenant" (Jer 31:31). The expression is translated in the Greek of the Septuagint as "new dispensation," "new testament" (*kainē diathēkē*). The message announced that God intended to establish a new covenant. The Christian faith sees this promise fulfilled in the mystery of Christ Jesus with the institution of the Eucharist (cf. 1 Co 11:25; Heb 9:15). Consequently, that collection of writings which expresses the Church's faith in all its novelty is called the "New Testament." The title itself points toward a relationship with the "Old Testament."

A. The New Testament Recognizes the Authority of the Sacred Scriptures of the Jewish People

3. The New Testament writings were never presented as something entirely new. On the contrary, they attest their rootedness in the long religious experience of the people of Israel, an experience recorded in diverse forms in the sacred books which comprise the Jewish Scriptures. The New Testament recognizes their divine authority. This recognition manifests itself in different ways, with different degrees of explicitness.

1. Implicit recognition of authority

Beginning from the less explicit, which nevertheless is revealing, we notice that the same language is used. The Greek of the New Testament is closely dependent on the Greek of the Septuagint, in grammatical turns of phrase which were influenced by the Hebrew, or in the vocabulary, of a religious nature in particular. Without a knowledge of Septuagint Greek, it is impossible to ascertain the exact meaning of many important New Testament terms.[5]

This linguistic relationship extends to numerous expressions borrowed by the New Testament from the Jewish Scriptures, giving rise to frequent *reminiscences and implicit quotations,* that is, entire phrases found in the New Testament without any indication of origin. These reminiscences are numerous, but their identification often gives rise to discussion. To take an obvious example: although the Book of Revelation contains no explicit quotations from the Jewish Bible, it is a whole tissue of reminiscences and allusions. The text is so steeped in the Old Testament that it is difficult to distinguish what is an allusion to it and what is not.

What is true of the Book of Revelation is true also— although to a lesser degree—of the Gospels, the Acts of the Apostles and the Letters.[6] The difference is that in these writ-

---

5. For example, *angelos,* "messenger" or "angel"; *ginōskein,* "to know" or "to have relations with; *"diathēkē,"* "testament" or "pact," "covenant"; *nomos,* "law" or "revelation"; *ethnē,* "nations" or "pagans."

6. For example, in the Gospel of Matthew there are 160 implicit quotations and allusions; 60 in the Gospel of Mark; 192 in the Gospel of Luke; 137 in the Gospel of John; 140 in Acts; 72 in the Letter to the Romans, etc.

ings we find, in addition, many *explicit quotations,* that is, introduced as such.[7] In this way they clearly indicate the more important borrowings, recognizing thereby the authority of the Jewish Bible as divine revelation.

2. Explicit recourse to the authority of the Jewish Scriptures

4. This recognition of authority takes different forms depending on the case. Frequently, in a revelatory context the simple verb *legei* ("it says") is found without any expressed subject,[8] as in later rabbinic writings, but the context shows that a subject conferring great authority on the text is to be understood: Scripture, the Lord or Christ.[9] At other times the subject is expressed: it is Scripture, the Law, Moses or David, with the added note that he was inspired, the Holy Spirit or the prophet, frequently Isaiah, sometimes Jeremiah, but it is also the Holy Spirit or the Lord, as the prophets used to say.[10] Twice, Matthew has a complex formula indicating both the divine speaker and the human spokesperson: "what had been spoken by the Lord through the prophet..." (Mt 1:22; 2:15). At

---

7. There are 38 quotations in Matthew; 15 in Mark; 15 in Luke; 14 in John; 22 in Acts; 47 in Romans and so on.

8. Rm 10:8; Gal 3:16; Heb 8:8; 10:5.

9. Subjects understood: Scripture (Rm 10:8; cf. 10:11), the Lord (Gal 3:16; cf. Gn 13:14–15; Heb 8:8; cf. 8:8, 9), Christ (Heb 10:5).

10. Subjects expressed: "Scripture" (Rm 9:17; Gal 4:30); "the Law" (Rm 3:19; 7:7); "Moses" (Mk 7:10; Acts 3:22; Rm 10:19); "David" (Mt 22:43; Acts 2:25; 4:25; Rm 4:6); "the prophet" (Mt 1:22; 2:15); "Isaiah" (Mt 3:3; 4:14, etc., Jn 1:23; 12:39, 41; Rm 10:16, 20); "Jeremiah" (Mt 2:17); "the Holy Spirit" (Acts 1:16; Heb 3:7; 10:15); "the Lord" (Heb 8:8, 9, 10 = Jer 31:31, 32, 33).

other times the mention of the Lord remains implicit, suggested only by the preposition *dia* ("through"), referring to the human spokesperson. In these texts of Matthew, the verb "to say" in the present tense results in presenting the quotations from the Jewish Bible as living words possessing perennial authority.

Instead of the verb "to say," the term frequently used to introduce quotations is the verb "to write," in the Greek perfect tense, expressing the permanent effect of a past action: *gegraptai* ("it has been written" or simply "it is written"). This *gegraptai* carries considerable weight. Jesus successfully counters the tempter in the first temptation by simply saying: "It is written: man does not live by bread alone..." (Mt 4:4; Lk 4:4), adding *palin* ("on the contrary") the second time (Mt 4:7) and *gar* ("for") the third time (Mt 4:10). This "for" makes explicit the weight of argument attributed to the Old Testament text, something already implicit in the first two. It can also happen that a biblical text is not definitive and must give way to a new dispensation; in that case, the New Testament uses the Greek aorist tense, placing it in the past. Such is the case with the Law of Moses regarding divorce: "Because of your hardness of heart [Moses] wrote *(egrapsen)* this commandment for you" (Mk 10:5; cf. also Lk 20:28).

5. Frequently, the New Testament uses texts of the Jewish Bible *for the sake of argument,* both with the verb "to say" and the verb "to write." Sometimes we find the expression: "for it says..."[11] or more often: "for it is written...." [12] The formulae "for it

---

11. Rm 9:15, 17; 1 Tm 5:18.
12. Mt 2:5; 4:10; 26:31, etc.

is written," "because it is written," "according to what is written" are very frequent in the New Testament; in the Letter to the Romans alone there are seventeen instances.

In his doctrinal arguments, the Apostle Paul constantly relies on his people's Scriptures. He makes a clear distinction between scriptural argumentation and "human" reasoning. To the arguments from Scripture he attributes an incontestable value.[13] For him the Jewish Scriptures have an equally enduring value for guiding the spiritual lives of Christians: "For whatever was written in former days was written for our instruction, so that by steadfastness and by the encouragement of the Scriptures we might have hope."[14]

The New Testament recognizes the definitive value of arguments based on the Jewish Scriptures. In the Fourth Gospel, Jesus declares that "Scripture cannot be annulled" (Jn 10:35). Its value derives from the fact that it is the "Word of God" (Jn 10:35). This conviction is frequently evident. Two texts are particularly significant for this subject, since they speak of divine inspiration. In the Second Letter to Timothy, after mentioning the "Sacred Scriptures" (2 Tm 3:15), we find this affirmation: "All Scripture is inspired by God and is useful for teaching, for reproof, for correction, and for training in righteousness, so that the man of God may be proficient, equipped for every good work" (2 Tm 3:16–17). Specifically referring to the prophetic oracles contained in the Old Testament, the Second Letter of Peter declares: "First of all you must understand this, that no prophecy of Scripture is a matter

---

13. 1 Co 9:8; Rm 6:19; Gal 3:15.
14. Rm 15:4; cf. 1 Co 10:11.

of one's own interpretation, because no prophecy ever came by human will, but men moved by the Holy Spirit spoke from God" (2 Pt 1:20–21). These two texts not only affirm the authority of the Jewish Scriptures; they reveal the basis for this authority as divine inspiration.

B. The New Testament Attests Conformity to the Jewish Scriptures

6. A twofold conviction is apparent in other texts: on the one hand, what is written in the Jewish Scriptures must of necessity be fulfilled because it reveals the plan of God which cannot fail to be accomplished; on the other hand, the life, death, and resurrection of Christ are fully in accord with the Scriptures.

1. Necessity of fulfilling the Scriptures

The clearest expression of this is found in the words addressed by the risen Christ to his disciples in the Gospel of Luke: "These are my words that I spoke to you while I was still with you—that everything written about me in the Law of Moses, the Prophets, and the Psalms must *(dei)* be fulfilled" (Lk 24:44). This assertion shows the basis of the necessity *(dei,* "must") for the paschal mystery of Jesus, affirmed in numerous passages in the Gospels: "The Son of Man *must* undergo great suffering...and after three days rise again"[15]; "But how then would the Scriptures be fulfilled which say it *must* happen this way?" (Mt 26:54); "This Scripture *must* be fulfilled in me" (Lk 22:37).

---

15. Mk 8:31; cf. Mt 16:21; Lk 9:22; 17:25.

Because what is written in the Old Testament "must" be fulfilled, the events take place *"so that"* it is fulfilled. This is what Matthew often expresses in the infancy narrative, later on in Jesus' public life,[16] and for the whole passion (Mt 26:56). Mark has a parallel to the last mentioned passage in a powerfully elliptic phrase: "But let the Scriptures be fulfilled" (Mk 14:49). Luke does not use this expression but John has recourse to it almost as often as Matthew does.[17] The Gospels' insistence on the purpose of these events "so that the Scriptures be fulfilled"[18] attributes the utmost importance to the Jewish Scriptures. It is clearly understood that these events would be meaningless if they did not correspond to what the Scriptures say. It would not be a question there of the realization of God's plan.

2. Conformity to the Scriptures

7. Other texts affirm that the whole mystery of Christ is in conformity with the Jewish Scriptures. The early Christian preaching is summarized in the kerygmatic formula recounted by Paul: "For I handed on to you as of first importance what I in turn had received: that Christ died for our sins *in accordance with the Scriptures,* and that he was buried, and that he was raised on the third day *in accordance with the Scriptures,* and that he appeared..." (1 Co 15:3–5). He adds: "Whether, then, it was I or they, this is what we preach and this is what you believed" (1 Co 15:11). The Christian faith, then, is not

---

16. Mt 1:22; 2:15; 2:23; Mt 4:14; 8:17; 12:17; 13:35; 21:4.

17. Jn 12:38; 13:18; 15:25; 17:12; 19:24, 28, 36.

18. Mk 14:49; cf. Mt 26:56; Jn 19:28.

based solely on events, but on the conformity of these events to the revelation contained in the Jewish Scriptures. On his journey toward the passion, Jesus says: "The Son of Man goes as it is written of him" (Mt 26:24; Mk 14:21). After his resurrection, Jesus himself "interpreted to them the things about himself in all the Scriptures."[19] In his discourse to the Jews of Antioch in Pisidia, Paul recalls these events by saying that "the residents of Jerusalem and their leaders did not recognize him [Jesus] or understand the words of the prophets that are read every sabbath; they fulfilled these words by condemning him" (Acts 13:27). The New Testament shows by these declarations that it is indissolubly linked to the Jewish Scriptures.

Some disputed points that need to be kept in mind may be mentioned here. In the Gospel of Matthew, a saying of Jesus claims perfect continuity between the faith of Christians and the *Tôrâh:* "Do not think that I have come to abolish the Law or the Prophets; I have come not to abolish but to fulfill" (Mt 5:17). This theological affirmation is characteristic of Matthew and his community. It is in tension with other sayings of the Lord which relativizes the sabbath observance (Mt 12:8, 12) and ritual purity (Mt 15:11).

In the Gospel of Luke, Jesus appropriates a saying of Isaiah (Lk 4:17–21; Is 61:1–2) to define his mission as he begins his ministry. The ending of the Gospel expands this perspective when it speaks of fulfilling "all that is written" about Jesus (Lk 24:44).

---

19. Lk 24:27; cf. 24:25, 32, 45–46.

On that point, it is essential, according to Jesus, to "hear Moses and the prophets." The ending of the parable of the rich man and Lazarus (Lk 16:29–31) drives home the point: without a docile listening, even the greatest prodigies are of no avail.

The Fourth Gospel expresses a similar perspective: Jesus attributes to the writings of Moses an authority comparable to his own words, when he says to opponents: "If you do not believe what he wrote, how will you believe what I say?" (Jn 5:47). In a Gospel where Jesus affirms that his words "are spirit and life" (Jn 6:63), such an assertion gives primary importance to the *Tôrâh*.

In the Acts of the Apostles, the kerygmatic discourses of the Church leaders—Peter, Paul and Barnabas, James—place the events of the passion, resurrection, Pentecost and the missionary outreach of the Church in perfect continuity with the Jewish Scriptures.[20]

3. Conformity and Difference

8. Although it never explicitly affirms the authority of the Jewish Scriptures, the Letter to the Hebrews clearly shows that it recognizes this authority by repeatedly quoting texts to ground its teaching and exhortations. It contains numerous affirmations of conformity to prophetic revelation, but also affirmations of conformity that include aspects of non-conformity as well. This was already the case in the Pauline Letters.

---

20. Passion: Acts 4:25–26; 8:32–35; 13:27–29; resurrection: 2:25–35; 4:11; 13:32–35; Pentecost: 2:16–21; missionary outreach: 13:47; 15:18.

In the Letters to the Galatians and the Romans, the Apostle argues from the Law to prove that faith in Christ has put an end to the Law's regime. He shows that the Law as revelation predicted its own end as an institution necessary for salvation.[21] The most important text on this subject is Rm 3:21, where the Apostle affirms that the manifestation of the justice of God in the justification offered by faith in Christ is brought about "apart from the Law," but is nevertheless "attested by the Law and the Prophets." In a similar way, the Letter to the Hebrews shows that the mystery of Christ fulfills the prophecies and what was prefigured in the Jewish Scriptures, but, at the same time, affirms non-conformity to the ancient institutions: the glorified Christ is at one and the same time in conformity with the words of Ps 109(110):1, 4, and in non-conformity with the levitical priesthood (cf. Heb 7:11, 28).

The basic affirmation remains the same. The writings of the New Testament acknowledge that the Jewish Scriptures have a permanent value as divine revelation. They have a positive outlook toward them and regard them as the foundation on which they themselves rest. Consequently, the Church has always held that the Jewish Scriptures form an integral part of the Christian Bible.

C. Scripture and Oral Tradition in Judaism and Christianity

9. In many religions there exists a tension between Scripture and Tradition. This is true of Oriental religions (Hindu-

---

21. Gal 3:6–14, 24–25; 4:4–7; Rm 3:9–26; 6:14; 7:5–6.

ism, Buddhism, etc.) and Islam. The written texts can never express the Tradition in an exhaustive manner. They have to be completed by additions and interpretations which are eventually written down but are subject to certain limitations. This phenomenon can be seen in Christianity as well as in Judaism, with developments that are partly similar and partly different. A common trait is that both share a significant part of the same canon of Scripture.

1. Scripture and Tradition in the Old Testament and Judaism

Tradition gives birth to Scripture. The origin of Old Testament texts and the history of the formation of the canon have been the subject of important works in the last few years. A certain consensus has been reached according to which by the end of the first century of our era, the long process of the formation of the Hebrew Bible was practically completed. This canon comprised the *Tôrâh,* the Prophets and the greater part of the "Writings." To determine the origin of the individual books is often a difficult task. In many cases, one must settle for hypotheses. These are, for the most part, based on results furnished by form, tradition and redaction criticism. It can be deduced from them that ancient precepts were assembled in collections which were gradually inserted in the books of the Pentateuch. The older narratives were likewise committed to writing and arranged together. Collections of narrative texts and rules of conduct were combined. Prophetic messages were collected and compiled in books bearing the prophets' names. The sapiential texts, psalms and didactic narratives were likewise collected much later.

Over time Tradition produced a "second Scripture" (Mishna). No written text can adequately express all the riches of a tradition.[22] The biblical sacred texts left open many questions concerning the proper understanding of Israelite faith and conduct. That gave rise, in Pharisaic and Rabbinic Judaism, to a long process of written texts, from the "Mishna" ("Second Text"), edited at the beginning of the third century by Jehuda ha-Nasi, to the "Tosepta" ("Supplement") and Talmud in its twofold form (Babylonian and Jerusalem). Notwithstanding its authority, this interpretation by itself was not deemed adequate in later times, with the result that later rabbinic explanations were added. These additions were never granted the same authority as the Talmud; they served only as an aid to interpretation. Unresolved questions were submitted to the decisions of the Grand Rabbinate.

In this manner, written texts gave rise to further developments. Between written texts and oral tradition a certain sustained tension is evident.

The Limits of Tradition. When it was put into writing to be joined to Scripture, a normative Tradition, for all that, never enjoyed the same authority as Scripture. It did not become part of the "Writings which soil the hands," that is, "which are sacred," and was not accepted as such in the liturgy. The Mishna, the Tosepta and the Talmud have their place in the synagogue as texts to be studied, but they are not read in the liturgy. Generally, a tradition is evaluated by its conformity to the *Tôrâh.* The reading of the *Tôrâh* occupies a

---

22. According to rabbinic understanding, the written Law was duplicated by a complementary oral Law.

privileged place in the liturgy of the synagogue. To it are added pericopes chosen from the Prophets. According to ancient Jewish belief, the *Tôrâh* was conceived before the creation of the world. The Samaritans accept only the *Tôrâh* as Sacred Scripture, while the Sadducees reject every normative Tradition outside the Law and the Prophets. Conversely, Pharisaic and Rabbinic Judaism accept, alongside the written Law, an oral Law given simultaneously to Moses and enjoying the same authority. A tract in the Mishna states: "At Sinai, Moses received the oral Law and handed it on to Joshua, and Joshua to the ancestors, and the ancestors to the prophets, and the prophets handed it on to members of the Great Synagogue" *(Aboth* 1:1). Clearly, a striking diversity is apparent from the manner of conceiving the role of Tradition.

2. Scripture and Tradition in early Christianity

10. *Tradition gives birth to Scripture,* In early Christianity, an evolution similar to that of Judaism can be observed with, however, an initial difference: early Christians had the Scriptures from the very beginning, since as Jews, they accepted Israel's Bible as Scripture. But for them an oral tradition was added on, "the teaching of the apostles" (Acts 2:42), which handed on the words of Jesus and the narrative of events concerning him. The Gospel catechesis took shape only gradually. To better ensure their faithful transmission, the words of Jesus and the narratives were put in writing. Thus, the way was prepared for the redaction of the Gospels which took place some decades after the death and resurrection of Jesus. In addition, professions of faith were also composed, together with the liturgical hymns which are found in the New Testa-

ment Letters. The Letters of Paul and the other apostles or leaders were first read in the church for which they were written (cf. 1 Th 5:27), were passed on to other churches (cf. Col 4:16), preserved to be read on other occasions and eventually accepted as Scripture (cf. 2 Pt 3:15–16) and attached to the Gospels. In this way, the canon of the New Testament was gradually formed within the apostolic Tradition.

Tradition completes Scripture. Christianity has in common with Judaism the conviction that God's revelation cannot be expressed in its entirety in written texts. This is clear from the ending of the Fourth Gospel, where it is stated that the whole world would be unable to contain the books that could be written recounting the actions of Jesus (Jn 21:25). On the other hand, a vibrant tradition is indispensable to make Scripture come alive and maintain its relevance.

It is worth recalling here the teaching of the Farewell Discourse on the role of "the Spirit of truth" after Jesus' departure. He will remind the disciples of all that Jesus said (Jn 14:26), bear witness on Jesus' behalf (15:26), and lead the disciples "into all the truth" (16:13), giving them a deeper understanding of the person of Christ, his message and work. As a result of the Spirit's action, the tradition remains alive and dynamic.

Having affirmed that the apostolic preaching is found "expressed in a special way" *("speciali modo exprimitur")* in the inspired books, the Second Vatican Council observes that it is Tradition "that renders a more profound understanding in the Church of Sacred Scripture and makes it always effective" *(Dei Verbum* 8). Scripture is defined as the "Word of God committed to writing under the inspiration of the Holy Spirit";

but it is Tradition that "transmits to the successors of the apostles the Word of God entrusted by Christ the Lord and by the Holy Spirit to the apostles, so that, illumined by the Spirit of truth, they will protect it faithfully, explain it and make it known by their preaching" (*DV* 9). The Council concludes: "Consequently, it is not from Sacred Scripture alone that the Church draws its certainty about everything which has been revealed," and adds: "That is why both—Scripture and Tradition—must be accepted and venerated with the same sense of devotion and reverence" (*DV* 9).

The limits of the additional contribution of Tradition. To what extent can there be in the Christian Church a tradition that is a material addition to the word of Scripture? This question has long been debated in the history of theology. The Second Vatican Council appears to have left the matter open, but at least declined to speak of "two sources of revelation," which would be Scripture and Tradition; it affirmed instead that "Sacred Tradition and Sacred Scripture constitute a unique sacred deposit of the Word of God which is entrusted to the Church" (*DV* 10). It likewise rejected the idea of a tradition completely independent of Scripture. On one point at least, the Council mentions an additional contribution made by Tradition, one of great importance: Tradition "enabled the Church to recognize the full canon of the sacred books" (*DV* 8). Here, the extent to which Scripture and Tradition are inseparable can be seen.

3. Relationship between the two perspectives

11. As we have shown, there is a corresponding relationship between Scripture and Tradition in Judaism and Chris-

tianity. On one point, there is a greater correspondence, since both religions share a common heritage in the "Sacred Scripture of Israel."[23]

From a hermeneutical viewpoint, however, perspectives differ. For all the currents within Judaism during the period corresponding to the formation of the canon, the Law was at the center. Indeed, in it were to be found the essential institutions revealed by God himself governing the religious, moral, juridical and political life of the Jewish nation after the Exile. The prophetic corpus contains divinely inspired words, transmitted by the prophets and accepted as authentic, but it contained no laws capable of providing an institutional base. From this point of view, the prophetic writings are of second rank. The "Writings" contain neither laws nor prophetic words and consequently occupy third place.

This hermeneutical perspective was not taken over by the Christian communities, with the exception, perhaps, of those in a Judeo-Christian milieu linked to Pharisaic Judaism by their veneration of the Law. In the New Testament, the general tendency is to give more importance to the prophetic texts, understood as foretelling the mystery of Christ. The Apostle Paul and the Letter to the Hebrews do not hesitate to enter into polemics against the Law. Besides, early Christianity shared apocalyptic currents with the Zealots' and with the Essenes' apocalyptic messianic expectation; from Hellenistic Judaism it adopted a more extended, sapientially oriented body of Scripture capable of fostering intercultural relations.

---

23. The origin and extension of the canon of the Jewish Bible will be treated below in I, E, n. 16.

What distinguishes early Christianity from all these other currents is the conviction that the eschatological prophetic promises are no longer considered simply as an object of future hope, since their fulfillment had already begun in Jesus of Nazareth, the Christ. It is about him that the Jewish Scriptures speak, in their whole extension, and it is in light of him that they are to be fully comprehended.

D. Jewish Exegetical Methods Employed in the New Testament

1. Jewish methods of exegesis

12. Judaism derived from the Scriptures its understanding of God and of the world, as well as of God's plans. The clearest expression of how Jesus' contemporaries interpreted the Scriptures are given in the Dead Sea Scrolls, manuscripts copied between the second century B.C. and 60 A.D., and so are therefore close to Jesus' ministry and the formation of the Gospels. However, these documents express only one aspect of the Jewish tradition; they come from within a particular current and do not represent the whole tradition.

The earliest rabbinic attestation of exegetical method based on Old Testament texts is a series of seven "rules" traditionally attributed to Rabbi Hillel (d. 10 A.D.). Irrespective of whether this attribution is well founded or not, these seven *middoth* certainly represent a codification of contemporary methods of argument from Scripture, in particular for deducing rules of conduct.

Another method of using Scripture can be seen in first century historical writings, particularly Josephus, but it had already been employed in the Old Testament itself. It consists of using biblical terms to describe events in order to illuminate their meaning. Thus, the return from the Babylonian Exile is described in terms that evoke the liberation from Egyptian oppression at the time of the Exodus (Is 43:16–21). The final restoration of Zion is represented as a new Eden.[24] At Qumran, a similar technique was widely used.

2. Exegesis at Qumran and in the New Testament

13. With regard to form and method, the New Testament, especially the Gospels, presents striking resemblances to Qumran in its use of Scripture. The formulae for introducing quotations are often the same, for example: "thus it is written," "as it is written," "in conformity with what was said." The similarity in scriptural usage derives from an outlook common to both the Qumran community and that of the New Testament. Both were eschatological communities that saw biblical prophecies being fulfilled in their own time, in a manner surpassing the expectation and understanding of the prophets who had originally spoken them. Both were convinced that the full understanding of the prophecies had been revealed to their founder and transmitted by him, "the Teacher of Righteousness" at Qumran, Jesus for Christians.

Exactly as in the Dead Sea Scrolls, certain biblical texts are used in the New Testament in their literal and historical

---

24. Ezk 47:1–12 followed by Jl 2:18, 27 and Za 14:8–11.

sense, while others are applied in a more or less forced manner to the contemporary situation. Scripture was understood as containing the very words of God. Some interpretations, in both texts, take a word and separate it from its context and original meaning to give it a significance that does not correspond to the principles of modern exegesis. An important difference, however, should be noted. In the Qumran texts, the point of departure is Scripture. Certain texts—for example the *pesher* of Habakkuk—are an extended commentary on a biblical text, which is then applied, verse by verse, to a contemporary situation; others are collections of texts dealing with the same theme, for example, *11 Q Melchisedeq* on the messianic era. In the New Testament, in contrast, the point of departure is the Christ event. It does not apply Scripture to the present, but explains and comments on the Christ event in the light of Scripture. The only points in common are the techniques employed, often with a striking similarity, as in Rm 10:5–13 and in the Letter to the Hebrews.[25]

3. Rabbinic methods in the New Testament

14. Traditional Jewish methods of scriptural argumentation for the purpose of establishing rules of conduct—methods later codified by the rabbis—are frequently used in the words of Jesus transmitted in the Gospels and in the epistles. Those occurring most often are the first two *middoth* ("rules") of Hillel,

---

25. Heb 1:5–13; 2:6–9; 3:7—4:11; 7:1–28; 10:5–9; 12:5–11, 26–29.

qal wa-homer and *gezerah shawah.*[26] These correspond *more or less* to arguments *a fortiori* and by *analogy* respectively.

A particular trait is that the argument often revolves around the meaning of a single word. This meaning is established by its occurrence in a certain context and is then applied, often in a very artificial manner, to another context. This technique has a strong resemblance to rabbinic midrash, with one characteristic difference: in the rabbinic midrash, there is a citation of differing opinions from various authorities in such a way that it becomes a technique of argumentation, while in the New Testament the authority of Jesus is decisive.

Paul in particular frequently uses these techniques especially in discussions with well-informed Jewish adversaries, whether Christian or not. Oftentimes he uses them to counter traditional positions in Judaism or to support important points in his own teaching.[27]

---

26. *Qal wa-homer* is found in Mt 6:30; 7:11; Jn 7:23; 10:34–36; Rm 5:15, 17; 2 Co 3:7–11; *gezerah shawah* in Mt 12:1–4; Acts 2:25–28; Rm 4:1–12; Gal 3:10–14.

27. Cf. Gal 3:19 (Paul derives from the mediation of angels in the promulgation of the Law an argument to demonstrate the inferiority of the Law); 4:21–31 (the mention of Sarah and Hagar serves to demonstrate that Gentiles who believe in Christ are "children of the promise"); Rm 4:1–10 (it is the faith of Abraham, not circumcision, that justifies him); 10:6–8 (the verse that speaks of ascending the heavens is applied to Christ); 1 Co 10:4 (Christ is identified with the rock that accompanied the people in the desert); 15:45–47 (the two Adams, of whom Christ is the second and more perfect); 2 Co 3:13–16 (a symbolic meaning is attributed to the veil that covered Moses' face).

Rabbinic argumentation is also found in the Letters to the Ephesians and Hebrews.[28] The Epistle of Jude, for its part, is almost entirely made up of exegetical explications resembling the *pesharim* ("interpretations") found in the Qumran Scrolls and in some apocalyptic writings. It uses figures and examples in a verbal chain structure in conformity with Jewish scriptural exegesis.

A particular form of Jewish exegesis found in the New Testament is the homily delivered in the synagogue. According to Jn 6:59, the Bread of Life discourse was delivered by Jesus in the synagogue at Capernaum. Its form closely corresponds to synagogal homilies of the first century: an explanation of a Pentateuchal text supported by a prophetic text; each part of the text is explained; slight adjustments to the form of words are made to give a new interpretation. Traces of this model can perhaps also be found in the missionary discourses in the Acts of the Apostles, especially in Paul's homily in the synagogue of Pisidian Antioch (Acts 13:17–41).

4. Important allusions to the Old Testament

15. The New Testament frequently uses allusions to biblical events as a means of bringing out the meaning of the events of Jesus' life. The narratives of Jesus' infancy in the Gospel of Matthew do not disclose their full meaning unless read against the background of biblical and post-biblical narratives concerning Moses. The infancy gospel of Luke is more

---

28. Cf. Ep 4:8–9 (where a text on ascending the heavens, traditionally applied to Moses, is applied to Christ); Heb 7:1–28 (on the superiority of the priesthood according to Melchizedek over that of the levitical priests).

in the style of biblical allusions found in the first century Psalms of Solomon or in the Qumran Hymns; the Canticles of Mary, Zechariah and Simeon can be compared to Qumran hymns.[29] Events in the life of Jesus, like the theophany on the occasion of his baptism, the transfiguration, the multiplication of the loaves and the walking on the water, are similarly narrated with deliberate allusions to Old Testament events and narratives. The reaction of listeners to Jesus' parables (for example, the parable of the murderous tenants, Mt 21:33–43 and par.) shows that they were accustomed to using biblical imagery as a technique to express a message or give a lesson.

Among the Gospels, Matthew shows greatest familiarity with the Jewish techniques in utilizing Scripture. After the manner of the Qumran *pesharim*, he often quotes Scripture; he makes wide use of juridical and symbolic argumentation similar to those which were common in later rabbinic writings. More than the other Gospels, he uses midrashic stories in his narratives (the infancy gospel, the episode of Judas' death, the intervention of Pilate's wife). The rabbinic style of argumentation frequently used, especially in the Pauline Letters and in the Letter to the Hebrews, undoubtedly attests that the New Testament emerged from the matrix of Judaism and that it is infused with the mentality of Jewish biblical commentators.

E. The Extension of the Canon of Scripture

16. The title "canon" (Greek *kanōn,* "rule") means the list of books which are accepted as inspired by God and having

---

29. 1 QH 2:31–36; 5:12–16; 18:14–16.

a regulatory function for faith and morals. We are only concerned here with the formation of the canon of the Old Testament.

1. In Judaism

There are differences between the Jewish canon of Scripture[30] and the Christian canon of the Old Testament.[31] To explain these differences, it was generally thought that at the beginning of the Christian era, there existed two canons within Judaism: a Hebrew or Palestinian canon, and an extended Alexandrian canon in Greek—called the Septuagint—which was adopted by Christians.

Recent research and discoveries, however, have cast doubt on this opinion. It now seems more probable that at the time of Christianity's birth, closed collections of the Law and the Prophets existed in a textual form substantially identical with the Old Testament. The collection of "Writings," on the other

---

30. Jews count 24 books in their Bible, called TaNaK, a word formed from the initials of *Tôrâh,* "Law," *Nebi'im,* "Prophets," and *Ketubim,* other "Writings." The number 24 was often reduced to 22, the number of letters in the Hebrew alphabet. In the Christian canon, to these 24 (22) books correspond thirty-nine books, called "protocanonical." The numerical difference is explained by the fact that the Jews regarded as one book several writings that are distinct in the Christian canon (the writings of the Twelve Prophets, for example).

31. The Catholic Church accepts 46 books in its Old Testament canon, 39 protocanonical books and 7 deuterocanonical, so called because the former were accepted with little or no debate, while the latter (Sirach, Baruch, Tobit, Judith, Wisdom, 1 and 2 Maccabees and parts of Esther and Daniel) were accepted only after centuries of hesitation (on the part of certain Eastern Church Fathers as well as Jerome); the Churches of the Reformation call these "Apocrypha."

hand, was not as well defined either in Palestine or in the Jewish diaspora, with regard to the number of books and their textual form. Toward the end of the first century A.D., it seems that twenty-four (or twenty-two) books were generally accepted by Jews as sacred,[32] but it is only much later that the list became exclusive.[33] When the limits of the Hebrew canon were fixed, the deuterocanonical books were not included.

Many of the books belonging to the third group of religious texts, not yet fixed, were regularly read in Jewish communities during the first century A.D. They were translated into Greek and circulated among Hellenistic Jews, both in Palestine and in the diaspora.

2. In the early Church

17. Since the first Christians were for the most part Palestinian Jews, either "Hebrew" or "Hellenistic" (cf. Acts 6:1), their views on Scripture would have reflected those of their environment, but we are poorly informed on the subject. Nevertheless, the writings of the New Testament suggest that a sacred literature wider than the Hebrew canon circulated in

---

32. In *Contra Apion* (1:8), written between 93 and 95, Josephus comes very close to the idea of a canon of Scripture, but his vague reference to books to which titles had not yet been attached (later called the "Writings") shows that Judaism had not yet accepted a definitive collection of books.

33. The so-called Council of Jamnia was more in the nature of a school or an academy that sat in Jamnia between the years 75 and 117. There is no evidence of a decision drawing up a list of books. It seems that the canon of the Jewish Scriptures was not definitively fixed before the end of the second century. Scholarly discussion on the status of certain books continued into the third century.

Christian communities. Generally, the authors of the New Testament manifest a knowledge of the deuterocanonical books and other non-canonical ones since the number of books cited in the New Testament exceeds not only the Hebrew canon, but also the so-called Alexandrian canon.[34] When Christianity spread into the Greek world, it continued to use sacred books received from Hellenistic Judaism.[35] Although Hellenistic Christians received their Scriptures from the Jews in the form of the Septuagint, we do not know the precise form, because the Septuagint has come down to us only in Christian writings. What the Church seems to have received was a body of Sacred Scripture which, within Judaism, was in the process of becoming canonical. When Judaism came to close its own canon, the Christian Church was sufficiently independent from Judaism not to be immediately affected. It was only at a later period that a closed Hebrew canon began to exert influence on how Christians viewed it.

3. Formation of the Christian canon

18. The Old Testament of the early Church took different shapes in different regions as the diverse lists from Patristic

---

34. If the early Church had received from Alexandria a closed canon or a closed list of books, one would expect that the existing manuscripts of the Septuagint and the Christian lists of Old Testament books would be virtually the same. But this is not the case. The Old Testament lists of books of the Church Fathers and early councils do not have such unanimity. It was not the Alexandrian Jews who fixed the exclusive canon of Scripture, but the Church, beginning from the Septuagint.

35. These books comprised not only writings originally composed in Hebrew and translated into Greek, but also writings composed in Greek.

times show. The majority of Christian writings from the second century, as well as manuscripts of the Bible from the fourth century onward, made use of or contained a great number of Jewish sacred books, including those which were not admitted into the Hebrew canon. It was only after the Jews had defined their canon that the Church thought of closing its own Old Testament canon. But we are lacking information on the procedure adopted and the reasons given for the inclusion of this or that book in the canon. It is possible, nevertheless, to trace in a general way the evolution of the canon in the Church, both in the East and in the West.

In the East, from Origen's time (c. 185 – 253) there was an attempt to conform Christian usage to the Hebrew canon of twenty-four (or twenty-two) books using various combinations and stratagems. Origen himself knew of the existence of numerous textual differences, which were often considerable, between the Hebrew and the Greek Bible. To this was added the problem of different listings of books. The attempt to conform to the Hebrew text of the Hebrew canon did not prevent Christian authors in the East from utilizing in their writings books that were never admitted into the Hebrew canon, or from following the Septuagint text. The notion that the Hebrew canon should be preferred by Christians does not seem to have produced in the Eastern Church either a profound or long-lasting impression.

In the West, the use of a larger collection of sacred books was common and was defended by Augustine. When it came to selecting books to be included in the canon, Augustine (354 – 430) based his judgment on the constant practice of the Church. At the beginning of the fifth century, councils adopted his position in drawing up the Old Testament canon. Although these councils were regional, the unanimity expressed in their lists represents Church usage in the West.

As regards the textual differences between the Greek and the Hebrew Bible, Jerome based his translation on the Hebrew text. For the deuterocanonical books, he was generally content to correct the Old Latin (translation). From this time on, the Church in the West recognized a twofold biblical tradition: that of the Hebrew text for books of the Hebrew canon, and that of the Greek Bible for the other books, all in a Latin translation.

Based on a time-honored tradition, the Councils of Florence in 1442 and Trent in 1564 resolved for Catholics any doubts and uncertainties. Their list comprises seventy-three books, which were accepted as sacred and canonical because they were inspired by the Holy Spirit—forty-six for the Old Testament, twenty-seven for the New.[36] In this way the Catholic Church received its definitive canon. To determine this canon, it based itself on the Church's constant usage. In adopting this canon, which is larger than the Hebrew, it has preserved an authentic memory of Christian origins, since, as we have seen, the more restricted Hebrew canon is later than the formation of the New Testament.

---

36. Cf. DENZIGER-HUENERMANN, *Enchiridion Symbolorum,* 36th edition, Fribourg-im-Breisgau, Basil, Rome, Vienna, 1991, nn. 1334–1336, 1501–1504.

II

passed.[37] On th...
Testament a...
relationsh...
centur...
he ...
C...

Fundamental Themes in th[e
and Their Reception into Faith in ...

19. To the Jewish Scriptures which it received as the authentic Word of God, the Christian Church added other Scriptures expressing its faith in Jesus, the Christ. It follows then that the Christian Bible is not composed of one "Testament" but two "Testaments," the Old and the New, which have complex, dialectical relationships between them. A study of these relationships is indispensable for anyone who wishes to have a proper appreciation of the links between the Christian Church and the Jewish people. The understanding of these relationships has changed over time. The present chapter offers first an overview of these changes, followed by a more detailed study of the basic themes common to both Testaments.

A. Christian Understanding of the Relationships
between the Old and New Testaments

1. Affirmation of a reciprocal relationship

By "Old Testament" the Christian Church has no wish to suggest that the Jewish Scriptures are outdated or sur-

e contrary, it has always affirmed that the Old
d the New Testament are inseparable. Their first
p is precisely that. At the beginning of the second
, when Marcion wished to discard the Old Testament,
met with vehement resistance from the post-apostolic
Church. Moreover, his rejection of the Old Testament led him
to disregard a major portion of the New—he retained only the
Gospel of Luke and some Pauline Letters—which clearly
showed that his position was indefensible. It is in the light of
the Old Testament that the New understands the life, death
and glorification of Jesus (cf. 1 Co 15:3–4).

This relationship is also reciprocal: on the one hand, the
New Testament demands to be read in the light of the Old, but
it also invites a "rereading" of the Old in the light of Jesus
Christ (cf. Lk 24:45). How is this "rereading" to be done? It
extends to "all the Scriptures" (Lk 24:27), to "everything
written in the Law of Moses, the Prophets and the Psalms"
(24:44), but the New Testament only offers a limited number
of examples, not a methodology.

2. Rereading the Old Testament in the light of Christ

The examples given show that different methods were used,
taken from their cultural surroundings, as we have seen above.[38]

---

37. For the origin of this title, see above n. 2. Today in certain circles
there is a tendency to use "First Testament" to avoid any negative connotation attached to *"Old* Testament." But "Old Testament" is a biblical and
traditional expression which of itself does not have a negative connotation: the Church fully recognizes the importance of the Old Testament.

38. Cf. I, D: "Jewish Exegetical Methods Employed in the New
Testament," nn. 12–15.

The texts speak of typology[39] and of reading in the light of the Spirit (2 Co 3:14 –17). These suggest a twofold manner of reading, in its original meaning at the time of writing, and a subsequent interpretation in the light of Christ.

In Judaism, rereadings were commonplace. The Old Testament itself points the way. For example, in the episode of the manna, while not denying the original gift, the meaning is deepened to become a symbol of the Word through which God continually nourishes his people (cf. Dt 8:2–3). The Books of Chronicles are a rereading of the Book of Genesis and the Books of Samuel and Kings. What is specific to the Christian rereading is that it is done, as we have said, in the light of Christ.

This new interpretation does not negate the original meaning. Paul clearly states that "the very words of God were entrusted" to the Israelites (Rm 3:2), and he takes it for granted that these words of God could be read and understood before the coming of Christ. Although he speaks of a blindness of the Jews with regard to "the reading of the Old Testament" (2 Co 3:14), he does not mean a total incapacity to read, only an inability to read it in the light of Christ.

3. Allegorical rereading

20. The Hellenistic world had different methods which Christian exegesis made use of as well. The Greeks often interpreted their classical texts by allegorizing them. Commenting on ancient poetry like the works of Homer, where the gods seem to act like capricious and vindictive humans, schol-

---

39. Cf. Rm 5:14; 1 Co 10:6; Heb 9:24; 1 Pt 3:21.

ars explained this in a more religious and morally acceptable way by emphasizing that the poet was expressing himself in an allegorical manner when he wished to describe only human psychological conflicts, the passions of the soul, using the fiction of war between the gods. In this case, a new and more spiritual meaning replaced the original one.

Jews in the diaspora sometimes utilized this method, in particular to justify certain prescriptions of the Law which, taken literally, would appear nonsensical to the Hellenistic world. Philo of Alexandria, who had been nurtured in Hellenistic culture, tended in this direction. He developed, often with a touch of genius, the original meaning, but at other times he adopted an allegorical reading that completely overshadowed it. As a result, his exegesis was not accepted in Judaism.

In the New Testament, there is a single mention of "things spoken allegorically" (*allēgoroumena:* Gal 4:24), but here it is a question of typology, that is, the persons mentioned in the ancient text are presented as evoking things to come, without the slightest doubt being cast on their historicity. Another Pauline text uses allegory to interpret a detail of the Law (1 Co 9:9), but he never adopted this method as a general rule.

The Fathers of the Church and the medieval authors, in contrast, make systematic use of it for the entire Bible, even to the least detail—both for the New Testament as well as for the Old—to give a contemporary interpretation capable of application to the Christian life. For example, Origen sees the wood used by Moses to sweeten the bitter waters (Ex 15:22–25) as an allusion to the wood of the cross; he sees the scarlet thread used by Rahab as a means of recognizing her house (Jos 2:18) as an allusion to the blood of the Savior. Any detail capable of establishing contact between an Old Testament episode and Christian realities was exploited. In every page of the Old Testament, in addition, many direct and specific allusions to Christ and the Christian life were found, but there was a danger of detaching each detail from its context and severing the relationship between the biblical text and the concrete reality of salvation history. Interpretation then became arbitrary.

Certainly, the proposed teaching had a certain value because it was animated by faith and guided by a comprehensive understanding of Scripture read in the Tradition. But such teaching was not based on the commentated text. It was superimposed on it. It was inevitable, therefore, that at the moment of its greatest success, it went into irreversible decline.

4. Return to the literal sense

Thomas Aquinas saw clearly what underpinned allegorical exegesis: the commentator can only discover in a text what he already knows, and in order to know it, he had to find it in the literal sense of another text. From this Thomas Aquinas drew the conclusion: a valid argument cannot be constructed from the allegorical sense; it can only be done from the literal sense.[40]

Starting from the Middle Ages, the literal sense has been restored to a place of honor and has not ceased to prove its value. The critical study of the Old Testament has progressed

---

40. THOMAS AQUINAS, *Summa Theologica,* 1a, q. 1, a. 10ad 1um; cf. also *Quodl.* VII, 616m.

steadily in that direction, culminating in the supremacy of the historical-critical method.

And so an inverse process was set in motion: the relation between the Old Testament and Christian realities was now restricted to a limited number of Old Testament texts. Today, there is the danger of going to the opposite extreme of denying outright, together with the excesses of the allegorical method, all Patristic exegesis and the very idea of a Christian and Christological reading of Old Testament texts. This gave rise in contemporary theology, without as yet any consensus, to different ways of re-establishing a Christian interpretation of the Old Testament that would avoid arbitrariness and respect the original meaning.

5. The unity of God's plan and the idea of fulfillment

21. The basic theological presupposition is that God's salvific plan which culminates in Christ (cf. Ep 1:3–14) is a unity, but that it is realized progressively over the course of time. Both the unity and the gradual realization are important; likewise, continuity in certain points and discontinuity in others. From the outset, the action of God regarding human beings has tended toward final fulfillment, and consequently certain aspects that remain constant began to appear: God reveals himself, calls, confers a mission, promises, liberates, makes a covenant. The first realizations, though provisional and imperfect, already give a glimpse of the final plenitude. This is particularly evident in certain important themes which are developed throughout the entire Bible, from Genesis to Revelation: the way, the banquet, God's dwelling among men. Beginning from a continuous rereading of events and texts,

the Old Testament itself progressively opens up a perspective of fulfillment that is final and definitive. The Exodus, the primordial experience of Israel's faith (cf. Dt 6:20–25; 26:5–9), becomes the symbol of final salvation. Liberation from the Babylonian Exile and the prospect of an eschatological salvation are described as a new Exodus.[41] Christian interpretation is situated along these lines with this difference, that the fulfillment is already substantially realized in the mystery of Christ.

The notion of fulfillment is an extremely complex one,[42] one that could easily be distorted if there is a unilateral insistence either on continuity or discontinuity. Christian faith recognizes the fulfillment, in Christ, of the Scriptures and the hopes of Israel, but it does not understand this fulfillment as a literal one. Such a conception would be reductionist. In reality, in the mystery of Christ crucified and risen, fulfillment is brought about in a manner unforeseen. It includes transcendence.[43] Jesus is not confined to playing an already fixed role—that of Messiah—but he confers on the notions of Messiah and salvation a fullness which could not have been imagined in advance; he fills them with a new reality; one can even speak in this connection of a "new creation."[44] It would be wrong to consider the prophecies of the Old Testament as some kind of photographic anticipations of future events. All the texts, including those which later were read as messianic

---

41. Is 35:1–10; 40:1–5; 43:1–22; 48:12–21; 62.

42. Cf. below II, B, 9 and C, nn. 54–65.

43. *"Non solum impletur, verum etiam transcenditur,"* Ambroise Autpert, quoted by H. DE LUBAC, *Exégèse médiévale,* II, 246.

44. 2 Co 5:17; Gal 6:15.

prophecies, already had an immediate import and meaning for their contemporaries before attaining a fuller meaning for future hearers. The messiahship of Jesus has a meaning that is new and original.

The original task of the prophet was to help his contemporaries understand the events and the times they lived in from God's viewpoint. Accordingly, excessive insistence, characteristic of a certain apologetic, on the probative value attributable to the fulfillment of prophecy must be discarded. This insistence has contributed to harsh judgments by Christians of Jews and their reading of the Old Testament: the more reference to Christ is found in Old Testament texts, the more the incredulity of the Jews is considered inexcusable and obstinate.

Insistence on discontinuity between both Testaments and going beyond former perspectives should not, however, lead to a one-sided spiritualization. What has already been accomplished in Christ must yet be accomplished in us and in the world. The definitive fulfillment will be at the end with the resurrection of the dead, a new heaven and a new earth. Jewish messianic expectation is not in vain. It can become for us Christians a powerful stimulant to keep alive the eschatological dimension of our faith. Like them, we too live in expectation. The difference is that for us the One who is to come will have the traits of the Jesus who has already come and is already present and active among us.

6. Current perspectives

The Old Testament in itself has great value as the Word of God. To read the Old Testament as Christians does not mean wishing to find everywhere direct reference to Jesus and Christian realities. True, for Christians, all the Old Testament economy is in movement toward Christ; if then the Old Testament is read in the light of Christ, one can, retrospectively, perceive something of this movement. But since it is a movement, a slow and difficult progression throughout the course of history, each event and each text is situated at a particular point along the way, at a greater or lesser distance from the end. Retrospective rereadings through Christian eyes mean perceiving both the movement toward Christ and the distance from Christ, prefiguration and dissimilarity. Conversely, the New Testament cannot be fully understood except in the light of the Old Testament.

The Christian interpretation of the Old Testament is then a differentiated one, depending on the different genres of texts. It does not blur the difference between Law and Gospel, but distinguishes carefully the successive phases of revelation and salvation history. It is a theological interpretation, but at the same time historically grounded. Far from excluding historical-critical exegesis, it demands it.

Although the Christian reader is aware that the internal dynamism of the Old Testament finds its goal in Jesus, this is a retrospective perception whose point of departure is not in the text as such, but in the events of the New Testament proclaimed by the apostolic preaching. It cannot be said, therefore, that Jews do not see what has been proclaimed in the text, but that the Christian, in the light of Christ and in the Spirit, discovers in the text an additional meaning that was hidden there.

e horror in the wake of the extermination of the Shoah) during the Second World War has led all the Chu.   es to rethink their relationship with Judaism and, as a result, to reconsider their interpretation of the Jewish Bible, the Old Testament. It may be asked whether Christians should be blamed for having monopolized the Jewish Bible and reading there what no Jew has found. Should not Christians henceforth read the Bible as Jews do, in order to show proper respect for its Jewish origins?

In answer to the last question, a negative response must be given for hermeneutical reasons. For to read the Bible as Judaism does necessarily involves an implicit acceptance of all its presuppositions, that is, the full acceptance of what Judaism is, in particular, the authority of its writings and rabbinic traditions, which exclude faith in Jesus as Messiah and Son of God.

As regards the first question, the situation is different, for Christians can and ought to admit that the Jewish reading of the Bible is a possible one, in continuity with the Jewish Sacred Scriptures from the Second Temple period, a reading analogous to the Christian reading which developed in parallel fashion. Both readings are bound up with the vision of their respective faiths, of which the readings are the result and expression. Consequently, both are irreducible.

On the practical level of exegesis, Christians can, nonetheless, learn much from Jewish exegesis practiced for more than two thousand years, and, in fact, they have learned much in the course of history.[45] For their part, it is to be hoped that Jews themselves can derive profit from Christian exegetical research.

B. Shared Fundamental Themes

1. Revelation of God

23. *A God who speaks to humans.* The God of the Bible is one who enters into communication with human beings and speaks to them. In different ways, the Bible describes the initiative taken by God to communicate with humanity in choosing the people of Israel. God makes his word heard either directly or though a spokesperson.

In the Old Testament, God manifests himself to Israel as the One who speaks. The divine word takes the form of a promise made to Moses to bring the people of Israel out of Egypt (Ex 3:7–17), following the promises made to the patriarchs, Abraham, Isaac, and Jacob, for their descendants.[46] There is also the promise David receives in 2 Sm 7:1–17 concerning an offspring who will succeed him on the throne.

After the departure from Egypt, God commits himself to his people by a covenant in which he twice takes the initiative

---

45. Cf. the document of the Pontifical Biblical Commission, *The Interpretation of the Bible in the Church,* I, C, n. 2: "Approach through Recourse to Jewish Traditions of Interpretation."

46. Gn 12:1– 3; 26:23– 24; 46:2– 4.

(Ex 19—24; 32—34). In this setting, Moses receives the Law from God, often called *"words of God,"*[47] which he must transmit to the people.

As bearer of the word of God, Moses is considered a prophet,[48] and even more than a prophet (Nm 12:6–8). Throughout the course of the people's history, prophets were conscious of transmitting the word of God. The narratives of the prophetic call show how the word of God comes, forcefully imposes itself, and invites a response. Prophets like Isaiah, Jeremiah and Ezekiel perceive God's word as an event which changed their lives.[49] Their message is God's; to accept it is to accept the word of God. Even though it meets with resistance because of human freedom, the word of God is efficacious:[50] it is a force working at the heart of history. In the narrative of the creation of the world by God (Gn 1), we discover that, for God, to say is to do.

The New Testament prolongs this perspective and deepens it. For Jesus becomes the preacher of the Word of God (Lk 5:1) and appeals to Scripture: he is recognized as a prophet,[51] but he is more than a prophet. In the Fourth Gospel, the role of Jesus is distinguished from that of John the Baptist by opposing the earthly origin of the latter to the heavenly origin of the former: "The one who comes from above...testifies to what he has seen and heard.... He whom God has sent speaks

---

47. Ex 20:1; 24:3–8; 34:27–28; cf. Nm 15:31.

48. Hos 12:14; Dt 18:15, 18.

49. Is 6:5–8; Jer 1:4–10; Ez 2:1—3:3.

50. Is 55:11; Jer 20:9.

51. Mt 21:11, 46; Lk 7:16; 24:19; Jn 4:19; 6:14; 7:40; 9:17.

the words of God" (Jn 3:31, 32, 34). Jesus is not simply a messenger; he makes plain his intimacy with God. To understand Jesus' mission is to know his divine status: "I have not spoken on my own," Jesus says; "what I speak, I speak just as the Father has told me" (Jn 12:49, 50). Beginning from this bond which unites Jesus to the Father, the Fourth Gospel confesses Jesus as the *Logos,* "the Word" which "became flesh" (Jn 1:14).

The opening of the Letter to the Hebrews perfectly summarizes the way that has been traversed: God who "spoke long ago to our ancestors by the prophets," "has spoken to us by a Son" (Hb 1:1– 2), this Jesus of whom the Gospels and the apostolic preaching speak.

24. *God is One.* The strongest affirmation of the Jewish faith is that of Dt 6:4: "Hear, O Israel, the LORD our God is ONE LORD," which may not be separated from its consequences for the faithful: "You shall love the LORD your God with all your heart, with all your soul and all your might" (Dt 6:5).[52] The one God of Israel, the LORD, will be acknowledged as the one God of all humanity at the end of time (Zc 14:9). God is ONE: this proclamation points to the language of love (cf. Sg 6:9). The God who loves Israel is confessed as unique and calls each one to respond to that love by a love ever total.

Israel is called to acknowledge that the God who brought it out of Egypt is the only one who liberated it from slavery.

---

52. The word LORD is usually put in capitals here since the Hebrew text has the unpronounced tetragrammaton YHWH, the proper name of the God of Israel. In reading, the Jews substituted other words, especially *'adonaï,* "Lord."

This God alone has rescued Israel, and Israel must express its faith in him by keeping the Law and through the cult.

The affirmation "The LORD is ONE" was not originally an expression of radical monotheism, for the existence of other gods was not denied as, for example, the Decalogue shows (Ex 20:3). From the time of the Exile, the faith affirmation tended to become one of radical monotheism formulated through expressions like "the gods are nothing" (Is 45:14) or "there is no other."[53] In later Judaism the profession of Dt 6:4 becomes one of monotheistic faith; it is at the heart of Jewish prayer.

In the New Testament the profession of Jewish faith is repeated by Jesus himself in Mk 12:29, quoting Dt 6:4–5, and by his Jewish questioner who quotes Dt 4:35. The Christian faith also affirms the oneness of God, for "there is no God but one."[54] This oneness of God is firmly held, even when Jesus is recognized as Son (Rm 1:3–4), united with the Father (Jn 10:30; 17:11). For the glory that comes from the one God is received by Jesus from the Father as the "only Son full of grace and truth" (Jn 1:14). To express the Christian faith, Paul does not hesitate to divide into two the profession of Dt 6:4 to say: "For us there is one God, the Father...and one Lord, Jesus Christ" (1 Co 8:6).

25. *God the Creator and providence.* The Bible opens with the words: "In the beginning God created the heavens and the earth" (Gn 1:1); this heading dominates the text of Gn 1:1—2:4(a) as well as the whole of Scripture which recounts the divine acts of power. In this opening text, the

---

53. Dt 4:35, 39; Is 45:6, 14.

54. 1 Co 8:4; cf. Gal 3:20; Jas 2:19.

affirmation of the goodness of creation is repeated seven times, becoming one of the refrains (Gn 1:4 – 31).

In different formulations, in different contexts, the affirmation of God as Creator is constantly repeated. Thus in the narrative of the Exodus from Egypt, God exercises power over the wind and the sea (Ex 14:21). In Israel's prayer, God is confessed as the one "who made heaven and earth."[55] The creative action of God is the foundation and assurance of the salvation to come, likewise in prayer (Ps 121:2), as well as in the pronouncements of the prophets, for example in Jer 5:22 and 14:22. In Is 40—55, this creative action is the basis of hope for a salvation to come.[56] The sapiential books give the creative work of God a central place.[57]

The God who creates the world by his Word (Gn 1) and gives human beings the breath of life (Gn 2:7), is also the one who shows solicitude toward every human being from the moment of conception.[58]

Outside the Hebrew Bible, the text of 2 Mc 7:28 should be mentioned, where the mother of the seven martyred brothers exhorts the last one in the following way: "I beg you, my child, to look at the heaven and the earth, and see everything that is in them and recognize that God did not make them out of things that existed." The Latin translation has creation *ex nihilo* (from nothing.) An interesting aspect of this text is that the creative action of God serves here to ground faith in the resurrection of the just. The same is true of Rm 4:17.

---

55. Ps 115:15; 121:2; 124:8; 134:3; 146:6.

56. Is 42:5; 44:24; 45:11; 48:13.

57. Pr 8:22– 31; 14:31; 17:5; Jb 38; Ws 9:1– 2.

58. Ps 139:13 –15; Jb 10:9 –12.

Faith in God the Creator, vanquisher of the cosmic forces and of evil, becomes inseparable from trust in him as Savior of the Israelite people as well as of individuals.[59]

26. In the New Testament, the conviction that all existing things are the work of God comes straight from the Old Testament. It seems so obvious that no proof is needed, and creation vocabulary is not prominent in the Gospels. Nevertheless, there is in Mt 19:4 a reference to Gn 1:27 which speaks of the creation of man and woman. More generally, Mk 13:19 recalls "the beginning of the creation that God created." Lastly, Mt 13:35(b), referring to parables, speaks of "what has been hidden from the foundation of the world."

In his preaching, Jesus frequently insists on the trust human beings should have in God on whom everything depends: "Do not worry about your life, what you will eat...or about your body, what you will wear.... Look at the birds of the air; they neither sow nor reap...and yet your heavenly Father feeds them."[60] The care of God the Creator extends to both good and bad, on whom "he makes his sun to rise" and to whom he sends rain to fructify the earth (Mt 5:45). The providence of God embraces all; for Jesus' disciples, this conviction ought to lead them to seek "first the kingdom of God and his righteousness" (Mt 6:33). In the Gospel of Matthew, Jesus speaks of "the kingdom prepared for you from the foundation of the world" (Mt 25:34). The world created by God is where the salvation of human beings takes place; it awaits a complete "regeneration" (Mt 19:28).

---

59. Jb 26:12–13; Ps 74:12–23; 89:10–15; Is 45:7–8; 51:9–11.
60. Mt 6:25–26; cf. Lk 12:22–32.

Beginning from the Jewish Bible, which affirms that God created all things by his word,[61] the prologue of the Fourth Gospel proclaims that "in the beginning was the Word," that "the Word was God," that "all things came into being through him," and "without him not one thing came into being" (Jn 1:1–3). The Word came into the world, yet the world did not know him (Jn 1:10). In spite of human obstacles, God's plan is clearly defined in Jn 3:16: "God so loved the world that he gave his only Son, so that everyone who believes in him may not perish, but may have eternal life." Jesus witnesses to this love of God to the very end (Jn 13:1). After the resurrection Jesus "breathes" on the disciples, repeating God's action in the creation of human beings (Gn 2:7), and suggesting that a new creation will be the work of the Holy Spirit (Jn 20:22).

Using a different vocabulary, the Book of Revelation offers a similar perspective. The creator God (Rv 4:11) is the originator of a plan of salvation that could not be realized except by the Lamb, "as if sacrificed" (Rv 5:6), accomplished in the paschal mystery by him who is "the origin of God's creation" (Rv 3:14). In history, the victory over the forces of evil will go hand in hand with a new creation that will have God himself as light,[62] and a temple will no longer be needed, for the Almighty God and the Lamb will be the Temple of the heavenly city, the new Jerusalem (Rv 21:2, 22).

In the Pauline Letters, creation has an equally important place. The argument of Paul in Rm 1:20–21 concerning the pagans is well known. The Apostle affirms that "since the

---

61. Ws 9:1; cf. Ps 33:6–9; Si 42:15.
62. Rv 22:5; cf. Is 60:9.

creation of the world, his eternal power and divine nature, invisible though they are, have been understood and seen through the things he has made," and so the pagans are "without excuse" in not giving glory to God and having "served the creature rather than the Creator" (Rm 1:25; cf. Ws 13:1–9). Creation will be freed "from its bondage to decay" (Rm 8:20–21). So creation then may not be rejected as evil. In 1 Tm 4:4, it is affirmed that "everything created by God is good, and nothing is to be rejected provided it is received with thanksgiving."

In the act of creation, the role attributed to Wisdom in the Old Testament is attributed in the New Testament to the person of Christ, the Son of God. Like the "Word" in John's prologue (1:3), it is a universal mediation, expressed in Greek by the preposition *dia,* which is also found in Heb 1:2. Associated with "the Father *from whom* are all things," it is Jesus Christ "*through whom* are all things" (1 Co 8:6). Developing this theme, the hymn of Col 1:15–20 affirms that "in him all things were created" and that "all things have been created through him and for him; he is before all things, in him all things hold together" (Col 1:16–17).

On the other hand, the resurrection of Christ is understood as the inauguration of a new creation, of a kind that "if anyone is in Christ, he is a 'new creation.'"[63] Faced with the proliferation of human sin, the plan of God in Christ was to bring about a new creation. We will take up this theme later after treating of the human condition.

---

63. 2 Co 5:17; cf. Gal 6:15.

2. The human person: greatness and wretchedness

a) In the Old Testament

27. It is commonplace to speak in one phrase of the "greatness and wretchedness" of the human person. These terms are not found in the Old Testament to characterize the human condition, but equivalent expressions are encountered: in the first three chapters of Genesis, man and woman are, on the one hand, "created in the image of God" (Gn 1:27), but are also "sent forth from the garden of Eden" (Gn 3:24) because they disobeyed the command of God. These chapters set the tone for reading the entire Bible. Everyone is invited to recognize therein the essential traits of the human situation and the basis for the whole of salvation history.

Created in the image of God: affirmed before the call of Abraham and the election of Israel, this characteristic applies to all men and women of all times and places (Gn 1:26–27)[64] and confers on them their highest dignity. The expression may have originated in the royal ideology of the nations surrounding Israel, especially in Egypt, where the Pharaoh was regarded as the living image of god, entrusted with the maintenance and renewal of the cosmos. But the Bible has made this metaphor into a fundamental category for defining every human person. God's words: "Let us make man in our image, according to our likeness, and let them have dominion over..." (Gn 1:26), show that human beings are creatures of God

---

64. Gn 5:1; Ws 2:23; Si 17:3. The same idea is found in Ps 8:5–7, although expressed differently.

whose task is to govern the earth that was created and populated by God. Insofar as they are images of God and the Creator's stewards, human beings become recipients of his word and are called to be obedient to him (Gn 2:15 –17).

Human beings exist as man and woman whose task is at the service of life. In the affirmation: "God created man in his image; in the image of God he created him; male and female he created them" (Gn 1:27), the differentiation of the sexes is paralleled with the relationship to God.

Furthermore, human procreation is closely associated with the task of governing the earth, as the divine blessing of the first human couple shows: "Be fruitful and multiply, and fill the earth and subdue it, and have dominion over..." (1:28). In this way, the likeness to God, the relationship of man and woman, and ruling over the world are intimately connected.

The close relationship between being created in God's image and having authority over the earth has many consequences. First of all, the universality of these characteristics excludes all superiority of one group or individual over another. All human beings are in the image of God and all are charged with furthering the Creator's work of ordering. Secondly, arrangements are made with a view to the harmonious coexistence of all living things in their search for the necessary means of subsistence: God provides for both humans and beasts (Gn 1:29 – 30).[65] Thirdly, human existence is endowed with a certain rhythm. As well as the rhythm of day and night, lunar months and solar years (Gn 1:14 –18), God

---

65. This ordinance is completed after the deluge, cf. Gn 9:3 – 4.

establishes a weekly rhythm with rest on the seventh day, the basis of the sabbath (Gn 2:1–3). When they keep the sabbath observance (Ex 20:8–11), the masters of the earth render homage to their Creator.

28. *Human wretchedness* finds its exemplary biblical expression in the story of the first sin and punishment in the garden of Eden. The narrative of Gn 2:4(b)—3:24 complements that of Gn 1:1—2:4(a) by explaining how, in a creation that was "good"[66] and with the creation of humans even "very good" (Gn 1:31), wretchedness is nevertheless introduced.

The narrative defines the task given to the man, "to till and keep" the garden of Eden (Gn 2:15), adding the prohibition not "to eat of the tree of the knowledge of good and evil" (2:16–17). This prohibition implies that serving God and keeping his commandments are correlatives of the power to subdue the earth (Gn 1:26, 28).

The man fulfills God's intentions first of all by naming the animals (2:18–20) and then in accepting the woman as God's gift (2:23). In the temptation scene, in contrast, the human couple ceases to act in accordance with God's demands. By eating the fruit of the tree, the woman and the man succumb to the temptation to be like God and to acquire a "knowledge" that belongs to God alone (3:5–6). The result is that they try to avoid a confrontation with God. But their attempt to hide themselves shows the folly of sin, because it leaves them in the very place where the voice of God can be heard (3:8). God's question which indicts the man: "Where are you?" suggests

---

66. Gn 1:4, 10, 12, 18, 21, 25.

that he is not where he ought to be: at the service of God and working at his task (3:9). The man and the woman perceive that they are naked (3:7–10), which means that they have forfeited trust in each other and in the harmony of creation.

By his sentence, God redefines the conditions of human living but not the relationship between him and the couple (3:17–19). On the other hand, the man is relieved of his particular task in the garden, but not of work (3:17–19, 23). He is now oriented toward the "soil" (3:23; cf. 2:5). In other words, God continues to give human beings a task. In order to "subdue the earth and have dominion over it" (1:28), man must now work (3:23).

Henceforth, "pain" is the constant companion of the woman (3:16) and the man (3:17); death is their destiny (3:19). The relationship between man and wife deteriorates. The word "pain" is associated with pregnancy and birth (3:16), and with physical and mental fatigue resulting from work as well (3:17).[67] Paradoxically, into what should be in themselves a source of profound joy, childbirth and productivity, pain is introduced. The verdict assigns "pain" to their existence on the "soil," which has been cursed because of their sin (3:17–18). Likewise for death: the end of human life is called a return "to the soil" from which the man was taken to fulfill his task.[68] In Gn 2—3, immortality seems to be dependent on existence in the garden of Eden and conditioned by respect for the prohibition of eating from the tree of "knowl-

---

67. Gn 5:29; Is 14:3; Ps 127:2; Pr 5:10; 10:22; 14:23.
68. Gn 3:19; cf. 2:7; 3:23.

edge." When this prohibition is violated, access to the tree of life (2:9) is henceforth blocked (3:22). In Wis 2:23–24, immortality is associated with likeness to God: "death entered the world through the devil's envy," and so a connection is established between Gn 1 and Gn 2—3.

Created in God's image and charged with cultivating the soil, the human couple have the great honor of being called to complete the creative action of God in taking care of his creatures (Wis 9:2–3). By refusing to heed the voice of God and preferring that of creatures, human freedom is brought into play; to suffer pain and death is the consequence of a choice made by the persons themselves. "Wretchedness" becomes a universal aspect of the human condition, but this aspect is secondary and does not abolish the "greatness" willed in God's plan for his creatures.

The chapters following in Genesis show to what level the human race can sink in sin and wretchedness: "The earth was corrupt in God's sight and was filled with violence.... All flesh had corrupted its ways upon the earth" (Gn 6:11–12), to such an extent that God decided on the deluge. But at least one man, Noah, together with his family "walked with God" (6:9), and God chose him to be the beginning of a new departure for humanity. From his posterity, God chose Abraham, commanding him to leave his country and promising "to make [his] name great" (Gn 12:2). The plan of God is now revealed as a universal one, for in Abraham "all the families of the earth shall be blessed" (12:3). The Old Testament reveals how this plan was realized through the ages, with alternating moments of wretchedness and greatness. Yet God was never resigned to leaving his people in wretchedness. He always reinstates them in the path of true greatness, for the benefit of the whole of humanity.

To these fundamental traits, it may be added that the Old Testament is not unaware of either the deceptive aspects of human existence (cf. Qo), the problem of innocent suffering (cf. especially Job), or the scandal of the persecution suffered by the innocent (cf. the stories of Elijah, Jeremiah, and the Jews persecuted by Antiochus). But in every case, especially the last, far from being an obstacle to human greatness, the experience of wretchedness, paradoxically, served to enhance greatness.

b) In the New Testament

29. The anthropology of the New Testament is based on that of the Old. It bears witness to the grandeur of the human person created in God's image (Gn 1:26–27) and to his wretchedness, brought on by the undeniable reality of sin, which makes him into a caricature of his true self.

Greatness of the human person. In the Gospels the greatness of the human being stands out in the solicitude shown to him by God, more than that of the birds of heaven or the flowers of the fields (Mt 6:30); it is also highlighted by the ideal proposed to him: to become merciful as God is merciful (Lk 6:36), perfect as God is perfect (Mt 5:45, 48). For the human being is a spiritual being who "does not live by bread alone, but by every word that comes from the mouth of God" (Mt 4:4; Lk 4:4). It is hunger for the Word of God that draws the crowds first to John the Baptist (Mt 3:5–6 and par.) and then to Jesus.[69] A glimpse of the divine draws them. As the

---

69. Mt 4:25 and par.; 15:31–32.

image of God, the human person is attracted toward God. Even the pagans are capable of great faith.[70]

It was the Apostle Paul who deepened anthropological reflection. As "apostle of the nations" (Rm 11:13), he understood that all people are called by God to a very great glory (1 Th 2:12), that of becoming children of God,[71] loved by him (Rm 5:8), members of the body of Christ (1 Co 12:27), filled with the Holy Spirit (1 Co 6:19). One can scarcely imagine a greater dignity.

The theme of the creation of the human person in God's image is treated by Paul in a multifaceted way. In 1 Co 11:7, the Apostle applies it to man, "who is the image and glory of God." Elsewhere, he applies it to Christ, "who is the image of God."[72] The vocation of the human person called by God is to become "conformed to the image of his Son, in order that he may be firstborn among many brothers" (Rm 8:29). It is by contemplating the glory of the Lord that this resemblance is bestowed (2 Co 3:18; 4:6). Begun in this life, transformation is achieved in the next, when "we will bear the image of the heavenly man" (1 Co 15:49). The greatness of the human person will then reach its culmination.

30. *The wretchedness of the human being.* The wretched state of humanity appears in various ways in the New Testament. It is clear that earth is no paradise! The Gospels repeatedly give a long list of maladies and infirmities that beset

---

70. Mt 8:10; 15:28.

71. Gal 3:26; 4:6; Rm 9:26.

72. 2 Co 4:4; cf. Col 1:15.

people.[73] In the Gospels demonic possession shows the abject slavery into which the whole person can fall (Mt 8:28 – 34 and par.). Death strikes and gives rise to sorrow.[74]

But it is especially moral misery that is the focus of attention. Humanity finds itself in a situation of sin that puts it in extreme danger.[75] Because of this, the invitation to conversion makes its presence felt. The preaching of John the Baptist reverberates with force in the desert.[76] Then Jesus takes up the cry: "he proclaimed the good news of God and said...'repent and believe in the good news'" (Mk 1:14 –15); "he went about all the cities and villages" (Mt 9:35). He denounced the evil "that comes out of a person" and "defiles" him (Mk 7:20). "For it is from within, from the human heart that evil intentions come: fornication, theft, murder, adultery, avarice, wickedness, deceit, licentiousness, envy, slander, pride, folly. All these evil things come from within and they defile a person."[77] In the parable of the prodigal son, Jesus described the miserable state to which the human person is reduced when he is far from his Father's house (Lk 15:13–16).

Jesus also spoke of persecutions suffered by people who dedicate themselves to the cause of "righteousness" (Mt 5:10) and predicted that his disciples would be persecuted.[78] He himself was (Jn 5:16); people sought to have him killed.[79] This

---

73. Mt 4:24 and par.; 8:16 and par.; 14:35 and par.; Jn 5:3.

74. Mk 5:38; Lk 7:12–13; Jn 11:33– 35.

75. Mt 3:10 and par.; Lk 13:1– 5; 17:26– 30; 19:41– 44; 23:29–31.

76. Mt 3:2 –12; Mk 1:2– 6; Lk 3:2– 9.

77. Mk 7:21– 23; cf. Mt 15:19– 20.

78. Mt 10:17– 23; Lk 21:12–17.

79. Mt 12:14 and par.; Jn 5:18; Mk 11:18; Lk 19:47.

murderous intention ended by bringing it about. The passion of Jesus was then an extreme manifestation of the moral wretchedness of humanity. Nothing was missing: betrayal, denial, abandonment, unjust trial and condemnation, insults and ill treatment, cruel sufferings accompanied by mockery. Human wickedness was released against "the Holy and Just One" (Acts 3:14) and put him in a state of terrible wretchedness.

In Paul's Letter to the Romans we find the most somber description of the moral decay of humanity (Rm 1:18—3:20), and the most penetrating analysis of the condition of the sinner (Rm 7:14–25). The picture which the Apostle paints of "all ungodliness and wickedness of those who by their wickedness suppress the truth" is truly overwhelming. Their refusal to give glory to God and to thank him leads to complete blindness and to the worst perversions (1:21–32). Paul wants to show that moral decay is universal and that the Jew is not exempt, in spite of the privilege of knowing the Law (2:17–24). He supports his thesis by a long series of texts from the Old Testament which declares that all people are sinners (3:10–18): "There is no one who is righteous, not even one."[80] This all-embracing negation is assuredly not the fruit of experience. It is more in the nature of a theological intuition of what humans become without the grace of God: evil is in the heart of each one (cf. Ps 51:7). This intuition of Paul is reinforced by the conviction that Christ "died for all."[81] Therefore, all have need of redemption. If sin were not universal, there would be some who would have had no need of redemption.

---

80. Rm 3:10; cf. Ps 14:3; Qo 7:20.
81. 2 Co 5:14; cf. Rm 5:18.

The Law did not bring with it a remedy for sin, for even if he recognizes that the Law is good and wishes to keep it, the sinner is forced to declare: "For I do not do the good I want, but the evil I do not want is what I do" (Rm 7:19). The power of sin avails of the Law itself to manifest its destructiveness all the more, by inciting transgression (7:13). And sin produces death[82] that provokes the sinner's cry of distress: "Wretched man that I am! Who will rescue me from this body of death?" (Rm 7:24) Thus is manifested the urgent need of redemption.

On a different note, but still quite forcefully, the Book of Revelation itself witnesses to the ravages of evil produced in the human world. It describes "Babylon," "the great prostitute," who has captivated "the kings of the earth" and "the inhabitants of the earth" in their abominations, and who is "drunk with the blood of the saints and of the witnesses to Jesus" (Rv 17:1–6). "Their sins are heaped high as heaven" (18:5). Evil releases terrible calamities. But it will not have the last word. Babylon falls (18:2). From heaven descends "the holy city, the new Jerusalem," "the abode of God among men" (21:2–3). The salvation that comes from God is opposed to the proliferation of evil.

3. God, Liberator and Savior

a) In the Old Testament

31. From the beginning of its history, with the *Exodus from Egypt*, Israel had experienced the LORD as Liberator and Savior: to this the Bible witnesses, describing how Israel was

---

82. Rm 5:12; 1 Co 15:56.

rescued from Egyptian power at the time of the crossing of the sea (Ex 14:21–31). The miraculous crossing of the sea becomes one of the principal themes for praising God.[83] Together with Israel's entrance to the promised land (Ex 15:17), the Exodus from Egypt becomes the principal affirmation of their profession of faith.[84]

One must be aware of the theological significance contained in the Old Testament formulations that express the Lord's intervention in this salvific event which was foundational for Israel: the LORD "led out" Israel from Egypt, "the house of slavery" (Ex 20:2; Dt 5:6); he "brought them up" to "a good and broad land, a land flowing with milk and honey" (Ex 3:8, 17); he "rescued" them from their oppressors (Ex 6:6; 12:27), he "ransomed" them as slaves are ransomed *(pâdâh:* Dt 7:8), or by exercising a right of kin *(gâ'al:* Ex 6:6; 15:13).

In the land of Canaan, continuing the experience of liberation from Egypt, Israel was once again the recipient of the liberating and salvific intervention of God. Oppressed by enemy peoples because of its infidelity toward God, Israel called to him for help. The Lord raised up a "judge" as "savior."[85]

In the anguished situation of the *Exile*—after the loss of the land—*Second Isaiah,* a prophet whose name is unknown, announced to the exiles an unheard of message: the Lord was about to repeat his original liberating intervention—that of the Exodus from Egypt—and even to surpass it. To the de-

---

83. Ex 15:1–10, 20–21; Ps 106:9–11; 114:1–5; 136:13–15.

84. Dt 26:6–9; cf. 6:21–23.

85. Jg 2:11–22; 3:9, 15; 2 Kg 13:5; Ne 9:27. The title "Savior" is given to God in 2 Sm 22:3; Is 43:3; 45:15; 60:16, as well as in other texts.

scendants of his chosen ones, Abraham and Jacob (Is 41:8), he would manifest himself as "Redeemer" *(gô'ēl)* in rescuing them from their foreign masters, the Babylonians.[86] "I, I am the Lord, and besides me there is no Savior; I declared and saved" (Is 43:11–12). As "Savior" and "Redeemer" of Israel, the LORD will be known to all men (Is 49:26).

After the return of the exiles, seen as imminent by Second Isaiah and soon to become a reality—but not in a very spectacular manner—the hope of *eschatological liberation* began to dawn: the spiritual successors of the exilic prophet announced the fulfillment, yet to come, of the redemption of Israel as a divine intervention at the end of time.[87] It is as Savior of Israel that the messianic prince is presented at the end of time (Mi 4:14 —5:5).

In many of the psalms, *salvation* takes on an *individual* aspect. Caught in the grip of sickness or hostile intrigues, an Israelite can invoke the Lord to be preserved from death or oppression.[88] He can also implore help from God for the king (Ps 20:10). He has confidence in the saving intervention of God (Ps 55:17–19). In return, the faithful, and especially the king (Ps 18 = 2 Sm 22), give thanks to the Lord for the help obtained and for the end of oppression.[89]

Furthermore, Israel hopes that the Lord will "redeem it from all its faults" (Ps 130:8).

In some texts, *salvation after death* makes its appearance. What, for Job, was only a glimmer of hope ("My redeemer

---

86. Is 41:14; 43:14; 44:6, 24; 47:4; 48:17; 49:7, 26; 54:5, 8.
87. Is 60:10–12; 35:9–10.
88. Ps 7:2; 22:21– 22; 26:11; 31:16; 44:27; 118:25; 119:134.
89. Ps 34:5; 66:19; 56:14; 71:23.

lives," Jb 19:25) becomes a sure hope in the psalm: "But God will ransom my soul from the power of Sheol, for he will receive me" (Ps 49:15). Likewise, in Ps 73:24 the psalmist says: "Afterward you will receive me in glory." God then can not only subdue the power of death to prevent the faithful from being separated from him, but he can also lead them beyond death to a participation in his glory.

The *Book of Daniel* and the *deuterocanonical writings* take up the theme of salvation and develop it further. According to apocalyptic expectation, the glorification of "the wise ones" (Dn 12:3)—no doubt, the people who are faithful to the Law in spite of persecution—will take their place in the resurrection of the dead (12:2). The sure hope of the martyrs' rising "for eternal life" (2 Mc 7:9) is forcefully expressed in the Second Book of Maccabees.[90] According to the *Book of Wisdom,* "people were taught...and were saved by wisdom" (Wis 9:19). The just man is a "son of God," so God "will help him and deliver him from the hand of his adversaries" (2:18), preserve him from death or save him beyond death, for "the hope" of the just is "full of immortality" (3:4).

b) In the New Testament

32. The New Testament follows the Old in presenting God as Savior. From the beginning of the Gospel of Luke, Mary praises God her "Savior" (Lk 1:47) and Zechariah blesses "the Lord, the God of Israel, because he has...redeemed his people" (Lk 1:68); the theme of salvation resounds four times in the "Benedictus"[91] with ever greater precision:

---

90. 2 Mc 7:9, 11, 14, 23, 29.
91. Lk 1:69, 71, 74, 77.

from the desire to be delivered from their enemies (1:71, 74) to being delivered from sin (1:77). Paul proclaims that the Gospel is "the power of God for salvation to everyone who has faith" (Rm 1:16).

In the Old Testament, to bring about liberation and salvation, God makes use of human instruments, who, as we have seen, were sometimes called saviors, as God himself more often was. In the New Testament, the title "redeemer" (*lytrōtēs*) appears only once and is given to Moses who is sent as such by God (Acts 7:35).[92] The title "Savior" is given to God and to Jesus. The very name of Jesus evokes the salvation given by God. The first Gospel draws attention to it early on and makes it clear that it has to do with spiritual salvation: the infant conceived by the virgin Mary will receive "the name Jesus, for he will save his people from their sins" (Mt 1:21). In the Gospel of Luke, the angels announce to the shepherds: "To you is born this day a Savior" (Lk 2:11). The Fourth Gospel opens up a wider perspective when the Samaritans proclaim that Jesus "is truly the Savior of the world" (Jn 4:42).

It can be said that in the Gospels, the Acts of the Apostles and in the uncontested Pauline Letters, the New Testament is very sparing in its use of the title Savior.[93] This reticence is explained by the fact that the title was widely used in the Hellenistic world; it was conferred on gods such as Asclepius,

---

92. In the Septuagint, *lytrōtēs* is found only twice, a title conferred on God: Ps 18(19):14; 77(78):35.

93. Applied to God, this title is found only once in the Gospels (Lk 1:47), never in Acts or in the uncontested Pauline Epistles; it is applied to Jesus twice in the Gospels (Lk 2:11; Jn 4:42), twice in Acts (Acts 5:31; 13:23), once in the uncontested Pauline Letters (Ph 3:20).

a healer god, and on divinized kings who were hailed as saviors of the people. The title, then, could become ambiguous. Furthermore, the notion of salvation in the Greek world had a strong individual and physical connotation, while the New Testament, in continuity with the Old, had a collective amplitude and was open to the spiritual. With the passage of time, the danger of ambiguity lessened. The Pastoral Letters and Second Peter use the title "Savior" often and apply it both to God and to Christ.[94]

In Jesus' public life, his power to save was manifested not only in the spiritual plane, as in Lk 19:9–10, but also—and frequently—in the bodily realm as well. Jesus cures sick people and heals them.[95] He observes: "It is your faith that has saved you."[96] The disciples implore him to rescue them from danger and he accedes to their request.[97] He liberates even from death.[98] On the cross his enemies mockingly recall that "he saved others," and they defy him to "save himself and come down from the cross."[99] But Jesus rejects a salvation of this kind for himself, because he has come to "give his life as

---

94. The First Letter to Timothy applies the title only to God, three times (1 Tm 1:1; 2:3; 4:10); the Second applies it only once to Christ (2 Tm 1:10); the Letter to Titus applies it three times to God (Ti 1:3; 2:10; 3:4) and three times to Christ (Ti 1:4; 2:13; 3:6). The Second Letter of Peter applies it only to Christ, together with the title "Lord" (2 Pt 1:1, 11; 2:20; 3:2, 18).

95. Mk 5:23, 28, 34; 6:56.

96. Mt 9:22 and par.; Mk 10:52; Lk 17:19; 18:42.

97. Mt 8:25 – 26 and par.; 14:30 – 31.

98. Mt 9:18 – 26 and par.; Lk 7:11–17; Jn 11:38 – 44.

99. Mt 27:39 – 44 and par.; Lk 23:39.

a ransom (*lytron:* means of liberation) for the many."[100] People wanted to make him a national liberator,[101] but he declined. He has brought salvation of a different kind.

The relationship between salvation and the Jewish people becomes an explicit object of theological reflection in John: "Salvation comes from the Jews" (Jn 4:22). This saying of Jesus is found in a context of opposition between Jewish and Samaritan cults that will become obsolete with the introduction of adoration "in spirit and truth" (4:23). At the end of the episode, the Samaritans acknowledge Jesus as "the Savior of the world" (Jn 4:42).

The title "Savior" is above all attributed to the risen Jesus, for, by his resurrection, "God exalted him at his right hand as Leader and Savior that he might give repentance and forgiveness of sins" (Acts 5:31). "There is salvation in no other" (4:12). The perspective is eschatological. "Save yourselves," Peter said, "from this corrupt generation" (Acts 2:40), and Paul presents the risen Jesus to Gentile converts as the one "who rescues us from the wrath that is coming" (1 Th 1:10). "Now that we have been justified by his blood, much more surely will we be saved through him from the wrath" (Rm 5:9).

This salvation was promised to the Israelite people, but the "nations" can also participate since the Gospel is "the power of God for salvation to everyone who has faith, to the Jew first, and also the Greek."[102] The hope of salvation, ex-

---

100. Mt 20:28; Mk 10:45.
101. Jn 6:15; Lk 24:21; Acts 1:6.
102. Rm 1:16; cf. 10:9–13; 15:8–12.

pressed so often and so forcefully in the Old Testament, finds its fulfillment in the New.

4. The election of Israel

a) In the Old Testament

33. God is the Liberator and Savior, above all, of an insignificant people—situated along with others between two great empires—because he has chosen this people for himself, setting them apart for a special relationship with him and for a mission in the world. The idea of election is fundamental for an understanding of the Old Testament and indeed for the whole Bible.

The affirmation that the LORD has "chosen" *(bāchar)* Israel is one of the more important teachings of Deuteronomy. The choice which the Lord made of Israel is manifest in the divine intervention to free it from Egypt and in the gift of the land. Deuteronomy explicitly denies that the divine choice was motivated by Israel's greatness or its moral perfection: "Know that the LORD your God is not giving you this good land to occupy because of your righteousness; for you are a stubborn people" (9:6). The only basis for God's choice was his love and faithfulness: "It is because he loved you and kept the oath that he swore to your ancestors" (7:8).

Chosen by God, Israel is called a *"holy people"* (Dt 7:6; 14:2). The word "holy" *(qādôš)* expresses, negatively, a separation from what is profane and, positively, a consecration to God's service. By using the expression "holy people," Deuteronomy emphasizes Israel's unique situation, a nation introduced into the domain of the sacred, having become the special possession of God and the object of his special protection. At the same time, the importance of Israel's response to the divine initiative is underlined as well as the necessity of appropriate conduct. In this way, the theology of election throws light both on the distinctive status and on the special responsibility of a people who, in the midst of other peoples, has been chosen as the special possession of God,[103] to be holy as God is holy.[104]

In Deuteronomy, the theme of election not only concerns people. One of the more fundamental requirements of the book is that the cult of the Lord be celebrated in the place which the Lord has chosen. The election of the people appears in the hortatory introduction to the laws, but in the laws themselves, divine election is concentrated on one sanctuary.[105] Other books focus on the place where this sanctuary is located and narrow the divine choice to the election of one tribe and one person. The chosen tribe is Judah in preference to Ephraim,[106] the chosen person is David.[107] He takes possession of Jerusalem, and the fortress of Zion becomes the "City of David" (2 Sm 5:6−7); to it the ark of the covenant is transferred (2 Sm 6:12). Thus the Lord has chosen Jerusalem (2 Ch 6:5)—or more precisely, Zion (Ps 132:13)—for his dwelling place.

---

103. In Hebrew *segullah:* Ex 19:5; Dt 7:6; 14:2; 26:18; Ps 135:4; Ml 3:17.

104. Lv 11:44−45; 19:2.

105. Dt 12:5, 11, 14, 18, 21, 26; 14:23−25, etc.

106. Ps 78:67−68; 1 Ch 28:4.

107. 2 Sm 6:21; 1 Kg 8:16; 1 Ch 28:4; 2 Ch 6:6; Ps 78:70.

For the Israelites in troubled and difficult times, when the future seemed closed, the conviction of being God's chosen people sustained their hope in the mercy of God and in fidelity to his promises. During the Exile, Second Isaiah takes up the theme of election[108] to console the exiles who thought they were abandoned by God (Is 49:14). The execution of God's justice had not brought an end to Israel's election; this remained solid, because it was founded on the election of the patriarchs.[109] To the idea of election, Second Isaiah attached the idea of service in presenting Israel as "the servant of the LORD"[110] destined to be "the light of the nations" (49:6). These texts clearly show that election, the basis of hope, brings with it a responsibility: Israel is to be, before the nations, the "witness" to the one God.[111] In bearing this witness, the servant will come to know the LORD as he is (43:10).

The election of Israel does not imply the rejection of the other nations. On the contrary, the presupposition is that the other nations also belong to God, for "the earth belongs to the Lord with all that is in it" (Dt 10:14), and God "apportioned the nations their patrimony" (32:8). When Israel is called by God "my firstborn son" (Ex 4:22; Jer 31:9) and "the firstfruits of the harvest" (Jer 2:3), these metaphors imply that other nations are equally part of God's family and harvest. This understanding of election is typical of the Bible as a whole.

---

108. Is 41:8–9; 44:1–2.
109. Is 41:8–9; 44:1–2.
110. Is 41:8–9; 43:10; 44:1–2; 45:4; 49:3.
111. Is 43:10, 12; 44:8; 55:5.

34. In its teaching on Israel's election, Deuteronomy, as we have said, puts the accent on the divine initiative, but also on the demands of the relationship between God and his people. Faith in the election could, nevertheless, harden into a proud superiority. The prophets battled against this deviation. A message of Amos relativizes the election and attributes to the nations the privilege of an exodus comparable to Israel's (Am 9:7). Another message says that election brings with it, on God's part, a greater severity: "You only have I known of all the families of the earth; therefore I will punish you for all your iniquities" (Am 3:2). Amos believes that the Lord had chosen Israel in a unique and special manner. In the context, the verb "to know" has a more profound and intimate meaning than consciousness of existence. It expresses a personal relationship more intimate than simply intellectual knowledge. But this relationship brings with it specific moral demands. Because it is God's people, Israel must live as God's people. If it fails in this duty, it will receive a "visit" of divine justice harsher than that of the other nations.

For Amos, it is clear that election means *responsibility* more than *privilege*. Obviously, the choice comes first followed by the demand. It is nonetheless true that God's election of Israel implies a high level of responsibility. By recalling this, the prophet disposes of the illusion that being God's chosen people means having a claim on God.

The peoples' and their kings' obstinate disobedience provoked the catastrophe of the Exile as foretold by the prophets. "The LORD said: I will also remove Judah out of my sight as I have removed Israel; I will reject this city that I have chosen, Jerusalem, and the house of which I said, 'My name shall be there'" (2 Kg 23:27). This decree of God produced its effect (2 Kg 25:1–21). But at the very moment when it was said: "The two families that the LORD chose have been rejected by him" (Jer 33:24), the Lord formally contradicts it: "I will restore their fortunes and will have mercy on them" (Jer 33:26). The prophet Hosea had already announced that at a time when Israel had become for God "Not-my-people" (Hos 1:8), God will say: "You are my people" (Hos 2:25). Jerusalem must be rebuilt; the prophet Haggai predicts for the rebuilt Temple a glory greater than that of Solomon's Temple (Hg 2:9). In this way, the election was solemnly reconfirmed.

b) In the New Testament

35. The expression "chosen people" is not found in the Gospels, but the conviction that Israel is God's chosen people is taken for granted although expressed in other terms. Matthew applies to Jesus the words of Micah where God speaks of Israel as *my* people; God says of the child born in Bethlehem: "He will shepherd *my* people Israel" (Mt 2:6: Mi 5:3). The choice of God and his fidelity to his chosen people is reflected later in the mission entrusted by God to Jesus: he has only been sent "to the lost sheep of the house of Israel" (Mt 15:24). Jesus himself uses the same words to limit the first mission of the "twelve apostles" (Mt 10:2, 5–6).

But the opposition Jesus encounters from the leaders brings about a change of perspective. At the conclusion of the parable of the murderous vineyard tenants, addressed to the "chief priests" and "elders of the people" (Mt 21:23), Jesus says to them: "The kingdom of God will be taken away from you and given to a nation that will produce its fruits" (21:43).

This word does not mean, however, the substitution of a pagan nation for the people of Israel. The new "nation" will be, on the contrary, in continuity with the chosen people, for it will have as a "cornerstone" the "stone rejected by the builders" (21:42), who is Jesus, a son of Israel, and it will be composed of Israelites with whom will be associated in "great numbers" (Mt 8:11) people coming from "all the nations" (Mt 28:19). The promise of God's presence with his people, which guaranteed Israel's election, is fulfilled by the presence of the risen Lord with his community.[112]

In the Gospel of Luke, the canticle of Zechariah proclaims that "the God of Israel has visited *his people*" (Lk 1:68), and that the mission of Zechariah's son will be a "going ahead of the Lord" so as to "give *his people* knowledge of salvation through the forgiveness of their sins" (1:76–77). During the presentation of the child Jesus in the Temple, Simeon qualifies the salvation brought by God as "glory for your people Israel" (2:32). Later on, a great miracle performed by Jesus gives rise to the crowd's exclamation: "God has visited his people" (7:16).

Nevertheless, for Luke a certain tension remains because of the opposition encountered by Jesus. This opposition, however, comes from the people's leaders, not from the people themselves who are favorably disposed toward Jesus.[113] In the Acts of the Apostles, Luke emphasizes that a great number of Peter's Jewish listeners, on the day of Pentecost and follow-

---

112. Mt 28:20; cf. 1:23.
113. Lk 19:48; 21:38.

ing, accepted his appeal to repent.[114] On the other hand, the narrative of Acts underlines that, on three occasions, in Asia Minor, Greece and Rome, the opposition initiated by the Jews forced Paul to relocate his mission among the Gentiles.[115] In Rome, Paul recalls for the Jewish leaders Isaiah's oracle predicting the hardening of "this people."[116] Thus the New Testament, like the Old, has two different perspectives on God's chosen people.

At the same time, there is an awareness that Israel's election is not an exclusive privilege. Already the Old Testament announced the attachment of "all the nations" to the God of Israel.[117] Along the same lines, Jesus announces that "many will come from the east and west and take their place in the banquet with Abraham, Isaac and Jacob." [118] The risen Jesus extends the apostles' mission and the offer of salvation to the "whole world." [119]

Because of this, the First Letter of Peter, addressed mostly to believers converted from paganism, confers on them the titles "chosen people" [120] and "holy nation" [121] in the same manner

---

114. Acts 2:41, 47; 4:4; 5:14.

115. Acts 13:46; 18:6; 28:28. In the Gospel of Luke, the episode of Jesus' preaching at Nazareth already presents the same type of structure as Acts 13:42 – 45 and 22:21–22: Jesus' universal outlook provokes hostility on the part of his townspeople (Lk 4:23 – 30).

116. Acts 28:26 – 27; Is 6:9 –10.

117. Ps 47:10; 86:9; Zc 14:16.

118. Mt 8:11; Lk 13:29.

119. Mk 16:15 –16; cf. Mt 28:18 – 20; Lk 24:47.

120. 1 Pt 2:9; Is 43:21.

121. 1 Pt 2:9; Ex 19:6.

as those converted from Judaism. Formerly, they were not a people, henceforth they are the "people of God." [122] The Second Letter of John calls the Christian community whom he addresses as "the *chosen* lady" (v.1), and "your *chosen* sister" (v.13) the community from which it was sent. To newly converted pagans Paul does not hesitate to declare: "We know, brothers, beloved by God, that he has *chosen* you..." (1 Th 1:4). Thus, the conviction of partaking in the divine election was communicated to all Christians.

36. In the Letter to the Romans, Paul makes clear that for Christians who have come from paganism, what is involved is a participation in Israel's election, God's special people. The Gentiles are "the wild olive shoot," "grafted to the real olive" to "share the riches of the root" (Rm 11:17, 24). They have no need to boast to the prejudice of the branches. "It is not you that support the root, but the root that supports you" (11:18).

To the question of whether the election of Israel remains valid, Paul gives two different answers: the first says that the branches have been cut off because of their refusal to believe (11:17, 20), but "a remnant remains, *chosen* by grace" (11:5). It cannot, therefore, be said that God has rejected his people (11:1–2). "Israel failed to attain what it was seeking. The *elect* [that is, the chosen remnant] attained it, but the rest were hardened" (11:7). The second response says that the Jews who became "enemies as regards the Gospel" remain "beloved as regards *election,* for the sake of the ancestors"

---

122. 1 Pt 2:10; Hos 2:25.

(11:28), and Paul foresees that they will obtain mercy (11:27, 31). The Jews do not cease to be called to live by faith in the intimacy of God, "for the gifts and calling of God are irrevocable" (11:29).

The New Testament never says that Israel has been rejected. From the earliest times, the Church considered the Jews to be important witnesses to the divine economy of salvation. She understands her own existence as a participation in the election of Israel and in a vocation that belongs, in the first place, to Israel, despite the fact that only a small number of Israelites accepted it.

While Paul compares the providence of God to the work of a potter who prepares for honor "vessels of mercy" (Rm 9:23), he declines to say that these vessels are exclusively or principally the Gentiles; rather they represent both Gentiles and Jews with a certain priority for Jews: "He called us not from the Jews only, but also from the Gentiles" (9:24).

Paul recalls that Christ "born under the Law" (Gal 4:4) has become "a servant to the circumcised on behalf of the truth of God, in order that he might confirm the promises given to the patriarchs" (Rm 15:8), meaning that Christ not only was circumcised, but is at the service of the circumcised because God has made promises to the patriarchs which were binding. "As regards the Gentiles," the Apostle says "they glorify God for his mercy" (15:9) and not for his fidelity, for their entry into the people of God is not the result of divine promises; it is something over and above what is owed to them. Therefore, it is the Jews who will first praise God among the nations; they will then invite the nations to rejoice with the people of God (15:9[b]–10).

Paul himself recalls with pride his Jewish origins.[123] In Rm 11:1, he mentions his status as "an Israelite, a descendant of Abraham, a member of the tribe of Benjamin" as proof that God has not rejected his people. In 2 Co 11:22, he sees it as a title of honor parallel to his title as minister of Christ (11:23). It is true that in Ph 3:7, these advantages which were for him gains, he now "regards as loss, because of Christ." But the point he is making here is that these advantages, instead of leading to Christ, kept him at a distance from him.

In Rm 3:1–2, Paul affirms unhesitatingly "the superiority of the Jews and the value of circumcision." Because first and most important, "the oracles of God were entrusted to them." Other reasons are given later on in Rm 9:4–5, forming an impressive list of God's gifts and not only of promises: to Israelites belong "the adoption, the glory, the covenants, the Law, the worship, the promises and the patriarchs, and from them according to the flesh came the Messiah" (Rm 9:4–5).

Nevertheless, Paul immediately adds that it is not enough to belong physically to Israel in order to rank among the "children of God." Before all else it is necessary to be "children of the promise" (Rm 9:6–8), which, according to the Apostle's thinking, implies belonging to Christ Jesus, in whom "every one of God's promises is a Yes" (2 Co 1:20). According to the Letter to the Galatians, the "offspring of Abraham" can only be one which is identified with Christ and those who belong to him (Gal 3:16, 29). But the Apostle emphasizes that "God has not cast off his people" (Rm 11:2). Since "the root is holy" (11:16), Paul is convinced that at the end, God, in his

---

123. Rm 11:1; 2 Co 11:22; Gal 1:14; Ph 3:5.

inscrutable wisdom, will graft all Israel back onto their own olive tree (11:24); "all Israel will be saved" (11:26).

It is because of our common roots and from this eschatological perspective that the Church acknowledges a special status of "elder brother" for the Jewish people, thereby giving them a unique place among all other religions.[124]

5. The covenant

a) In the Old Testament

37. As we have seen, the election of Israel presents a double aspect: it is a gift of love with a corresponding demand. The Sinai covenant clearly shows this double aspect.

As with the theology of election, that of the covenant is from beginning to end a theology of the people of the LORD. Adopted by the LORD as his son (cf. Ex 3:10, 4:22 – 23), Israel was to live totally and exclusively for him. The notion of covenant then, by its very definition, is opposed to an election of Israel that would automatically guarantee its existence and happiness. Election is to be understood as a calling that Israel as a people is to live out. The establishment of a covenant demanded on Israel's part a choice and a decision every bit as much as it had for God.[125]

As well as being employed in the Sinai narrative[126] (Ex 24:3 – 8), the word *berît*, generally translated as "covenant," appears in different biblical traditions, in particular those of

124. Discourse of John Paul II in the synagogue of Rome, April 13, 1986: *AAS* 78 (1986), 1120.

125. Dt 30:15 – 16, 19; Jos 24:21 – 25.

126. Ex 19 – 24; 32–34; especially 19:5; 24:7 – 8; 34:10, 27 – 28.

Noah, Abraham, David, Levi, and levitical priesthood; it is regularly used in Deuteronomy and in the Deuteronomic History. In each context, the word has different nuances of meaning. The usual translation of *berît* as "covenant" is often inappropriate. For the word can also mean more generally "promise," which is also a parallel with "oath" to express a solemn pledge.

Promise to Noah (Gn 9:8–17). After the deluge, God tells Noah and his sons that he is going to establish a bond *(berît)* between them and all living creatures. No obligation is imposed on Noah or on his descendants. God commits himself without reserve. This unconditional commitment on God's part toward creation is the basis of all life. Its unilateral character, that is, without imposing obligations on another, is evident by the fact that this promise explicitly includes the animals ("as many as came out of the ark": 9:10). The rainbow is to be a sign of God's promise. As long as it continues to appear in the clouds, God will recall his "everlasting promise" to "all flesh that is on the earth" (9:16).

Promise to Abraham (Gn 15:1–21; 17:1–26). According to Gn 15, the LORD makes a promise to Abraham expressed in these terms: "To your descendants I give this land" (15:18). The narrative makes no mention of a reciprocal obligation. The unilateral character of the promise is confirmed by the solemn rite which precedes the divine declaration. It is a rite of self-imprecation: passing between the two halves of the slaughtered animals, the person making the promise calls down on himself a similar fate, should he fail in his obligations (cf. Jer 34:18–20). If Gn 15 were a covenant with reciprocal obligations, both parties would have to participate in the rite. But this is not the case: the LORD alone, represented by "a flaming torch," passes between the portions of animal flesh.

The notion of promise in Gn 15 is also found in Gn 17 joined to a commandment. God imposes a general obligation of moral perfection on Abraham (17:1) and one particular positive prescription, circumcision (17:10–14). The words: "Walk before me and be blameless" (17:1) connote a total and unconditional dependence on God. The promise of a *berît* follows (17:2) and includes promises of extraordinary fecundity (17:4–6) and the gift of the land (17:8). These promises are unconditional and differ from those of the Sinai covenant (Ex 19:5–6). The word *berît* appears seventeen times in this chapter, with a basic meaning of solemn promise, but envisaging something more than a promise: here an everlasting bond is created between God and Abraham together with his posterity: "I will be your God" (Gn 17:8).

Just as the rainbow is the sign of the covenant with Noah, circumcision is the "sign" of the promise for Abraham, except that circumcision depends on a human decision. It is a mark that identifies those who will benefit from God's promise. Those who do not bear that mark will be cut off from the people, because they have broken the bond (Gn 17:14).

38. *The covenant at Sinai.* The text of Ex 19:4–8 shows the fundamental importance of the covenant of God with Israel. The poetic symbolism used—"carry on eagles' wings"—shows clearly how the covenant is intimately connected with the great liberation begun at the crossing of the Red Sea. The whole idea of covenant depends on this divine initiative. The

redemption accomplished by the LORD at the time of the Exodus from Egypt constitutes forever the foundation for fidelity and docility toward him.

The one acceptable response to this act of redemption is one of continual gratitude, which expresses itself in sincere submission. "Now, if you obey my voice and keep my covenant..." (19:5a): these stipulations should not be regarded as a basis for the covenant, but rather as a condition to be fulfilled in order to continue to enjoy the blessings promised by the Lord to his people. The acceptance of the proffered covenant includes, on the one hand, obligations and guarantees, and on the other, a special status: "You shall be my treasured possession *(segullah)."* In other words: "You shall be for me a priestly kingdom and a holy nation" (19:5b, 6).

Ex 24:3–8 brings to fulfillment the establishment of the covenant announced in 19:3–8. The separation of the blood into two equal parts prepares for the celebration of the rite. Half of the blood is poured on the altar, consecrated to God, while the other half is sprinkled on the assembled Israelites who are now consecrated as a holy people of the LORD and preordained to his service. The beginning (19:8) and the end (24:3, 7) of this great event, the founding of the covenant, are marked by a repetition of the same formula of response on the part of the people: "Everything that the LORD has spoken, we will do."

This relationship did not last. Israel adored the golden calf (Ex 32:1–6). The narrative recounting this infidelity and its consequences constitutes a reflection on the breaking of the covenant and its re-establishment. The people have experienced the anger of God—he speaks of destroying them (32:10).

But the repeated intercession of Moses,[127] the intervention of the Levites against the idolators (32:26–29), and the people's repentance (33:4–6) secure a promise from God not to carry out his threats (32:14) and to agree instead to walk once more with his people (33:14–17). God takes the initiative in re-establishing the covenant (34:1–10). These chapters reflect the conviction that, from the beginning, Israel tended to be unfaithful to the covenant, but that God, on his part, always restored relations.

The covenant of course is only a human way of conceiving the relationship of God with his people. As with all human concepts of this kind, it is an imperfect expression of the relationship between the divine and the human. The objective of the covenant is defined simply: "I will be your God and you will be my people" (Lv 26:12; cf. Ex 6:7). The covenant must not be understood simply as a bilateral contract, for God cannot be obligated in the same way as human beings. Nevertheless, the covenant allows the Israelites to appeal to God's fidelity. Israel has not been the only one to make a commitment. The LORD commits himself to the gift of the land as well as his own beneficent presence in the midst of his people.

Covenant in Deuteronomy. Deuteronomy and the redaction of the historical books which depend on it (Jos—Kings), distinguishes between "the promise to the ancestors" concerning the gift of the land (Dt 7:12; 8:18) and the covenant with the generation of Horeb (5:2–3). This latter covenant is a promise of allegiance to the Lord (2 Kg 23:1–3). Destined by God to be permanent (Dt 7:9, 12), it demands the people's

---

127. Ex 32:11–13, 31–32; 33:12–16; 34:9.

fidelity. The word *berît* often occurs with specific reference to the Decalogue rather than to the relationship between the Lord and Israel of which the Decalogue is a part: The Lord "declared to you his *berît,* that is, the ten commandments, which he charged you to observe."[128]

The declaration of Dt 5:3 merits particular attention, for it affirms the validity of the covenant for the present generation (cf. also 29:14). This verse gives a kind of key to interpreting the whole book. The temporal distance between the generations is abolished. The covenant at Sinai is made contemporaneous; it has been made "with us who are all alive here today."

Promise to David. This *berît* is along the same lines as those made with Noah and Abraham: a promise of God without a corresponding obligation for the king. David and his house from now on enjoy the favor of God who commits himself by oath to an "eternal covenant."[129] The nature of this covenant is defined by the words of God: "I will be a father to him and he shall be a son to me."[130]

Being an unconditional promise, the covenant with the house of David cannot be broken (Ps 89:29–38). If David's successor sins, God will punish him like a father punishes his sons, but he will not withdraw his favor (2 Sm 7:14–15). The perspective is very different from that of the Sinai covenant, where the divine favor is conditional: it requires obedience to the covenant on Israel's part (Ex 19:5–6).

---

128. Dt 4:13; cf. 4:23; 9:9, 11, 15.
129. Ps 89:4; 132:11; 2 Sm 23:5; Ps 89:29–30, 35.
130. 2 Sm 7:14 and par.; Ps 2:7; 89:28.

39. *A new covenant in Jer 31:31–34.* In Jeremiah's time, Israel's inability to keep the Sinai covenant was manifested in a tragic manner, resulting in the capture of Jerusalem and the destruction of the Temple. But God's fidelity toward his people is now manifested in the promise of a "new covenant," which the Lord says "will not be like the covenant that I made with their ancestors, when I took them by the hand to bring them out of Egypt; a covenant that they broke" (Jer 31:32). Coming after the breaking of the Sinai covenant, the new covenant makes possible a new beginning for the people of God. The prophetic message does not announce a change of law, but a new relationship with the Law of God, an interiorization. Instead of being written on "tablets of stone,"[131] the Law will be written by God on their "hearts" (Jer 31:33), which will guarantee a perfect obedience, willingly embraced, instead of the continual disobedience of the past.[132] The result will be a true reciprocal belonging, a personal relationship of each one with the Lord, which will make exhortation superfluous, something that had been so necessary in the past and yet so ineffectual, as the prophets had learned from bitter experience. This stupendous innovation will be based on the Lord's gratuitous initiative: a pardon granted to the people's faults.

The expression "new covenant" is not encountered elsewhere in the Old Testament, but a prophetic message in the Book of Ezekiel develops Jer 31:31–34, by announcing to the

---

131. Ex 24:12; 31:18, etc.
132. Is 1:1–31; Jer 7:25–26; 11:7–8.

house of Israel the gift of a "new heart" and a "new spirit," which will be the Spirit of God and will ensure submission to the Law of God.[133]

In Second Temple Judaism, certain Israelites saw the "new covenant"[134] realized in their own community, as a result of a more exact observance of the Law of Moses, according to the instructions of a "Teacher of Righteousness." This shows that the oracle of the Book of Jeremiah commanded attention at the time of Jesus and Paul. It will not be surprising then to see the expression "new covenant" repeated many times in the New Testament.

b) In the New Testament

40. The theme of God's covenant with his people in the writings of the New Testament is placed in a context of fulfillment, that is, in a fundamental progressive continuity, which necessarily involves breaks at certain points.

Continuity concerns above all the covenant relationship, while the breaks concern the Old Testament institutions that were supposed to establish and maintain that relationship. In the New Testament, the covenant is established on a new foundation, the person and work of Christ Jesus; the covenant relationship is deepened and broadened, opened to all through Christian faith.

The Synoptic Gospels and the Acts of the Apostles make little mention of the covenant. In the infancy gospels, the canticle of Zechariah (Lk 1:72) proclaims the fulfillment of

---

133. Ezk 36:26 – 27; cf. 11:19 – 20; 16:60; 37:26.

134. *Damascus Document,* 6:19; 19:33 – 34.

the covenant-promise given by God to Abraham for his descendants. The promise envisages the establishment of a reciprocal relationship (Lk 1:73–74) between God and those descendants.

At the Last Supper, Jesus intervened decisively in making his blood "the blood of the covenant" (Mt 26:28; Mk 14:24), the foundation of the "new covenant" (Lk 22:20; 1 Co 11:25). The expression "blood of the covenant" recalls the ratification of the Sinai covenant by Moses (Ex 24:8), suggesting continuity with that covenant. But the words of Jesus also reveal a radical newness, for, whereas the Sinai covenant included a ritual of sprinkling with the blood of sacrificed animals, Christ's covenant is founded on the blood of a human being who transforms his death as a condemned man into a generous gift, and thereby makes this rupture into a covenant event.

By "new covenant," Paul and Luke make this newness explicit. Yet, it is in continuity with another Old Testament text, the prophetic message of Jer 31:31–34, which announced that God would establish a "new covenant." The words of Jesus over the cup proclaim that the prophecy in the Book of Jeremiah is fulfilled in his passion. The disciples participate in this fulfillment by their partaking of the "supper of the Lord" (1 Co 11:20).

In the Acts of the Apostles (3:25), it is to the covenant promise that Peter draws attention. Peter addresses the Jews (3:12), but the text he quotes also concerns "all the nations of the earth" (Gn 22:18). The universal scope of the covenant is thereby expressed.

The *Book of Revelation* presents a characteristic development: in the eschatological vision of the "new Jerusalem" the covenant formula is employed and extended: "they will be his people and God himself will be with them" (21:3).

41. The *Letters of Paul* discuss the issue of the covenant more than once. The "new covenant" founded on the blood of Christ (1 Co 11:25) has a vertical dimension of union with the Lord through the "communion with the blood of Christ" (1 Co 10:6) and a horizontal dimension of the union of all Christians in "one body" (1 Co 10:17).

The apostolic ministry is at the service of the "new covenant" (2 Co 3:6), which is not "of the letter," like that of Sinai, but "of the Spirit," in accordance with the prophecies which promised that God would write his Law "on their hearts" (Jer 31:33) and give "a new spirit" that would be his Spirit.[135] Paul mentions more than once the covenant-law of Sinai[136]; he contrasts it with the covenant-promise of Abraham. The covenant-law is later and provisional (Gal 3:19 – 25). The covenant-promise is prior and definitive (Gal 3:16–18). From the beginning it has a universal openness.[137] It finds its fulfillment in Christ.[138]

Paul opposes the covenant-law of Sinai, on the one hand, to the extent that it competes with faith in Christ ("a person is justified not by works of the Law, but through faith in Jesus Christ": Gal 2:16; Rm 3:28), and on the other, insofar as it is a legal system of a particular people, which should not be imposed on believers coming from the "nations." But Paul af-

---

135. Ezk 36:26 – 28; Jl 3:1– 2.
136. Gal 3:15—4:7; 4:21– 28; Rm 6:14; 7:4– 6.
137. Gn 12:3; Gal 3:8.
138. Gal 3:29; 2 Co 1:20.

firms the value of revelation of "the old *diathēkē,*" that is to say, the writings of the "Old Testament," which are to be read in the light of Christ (2 Co 3:14–16).

For Paul, Jesus' establishment of "the new covenant in [his] blood" (1 Co 11:25) does not imply any rupture of God's covenant with his people, but constitutes its fulfillment. He includes "the covenants" among the privileges enjoyed by Israel, even if they do not believe in Christ (Rm 9:4). Israel continues to be in a covenant relationship and remains the people to whom the fulfillment of the covenant was promised, because their lack of faith cannot annul God's fidelity (Rm 11:29). Even if some Israelites have observed the Law as a means of establishing their own justice, the covenant-promise of God, who is rich in mercy (Rm 11:26–27), cannot be abrogated. Continuity is underlined by affirming that Christ is the end and the fulfillment to which the Law was leading the people of God (Gal 3:24). For many Jews, the veil with which Moses covered his face remains over the Old Testament (2 Co 3:13, 15), thus preventing them from recognizing Christ's revelation there. This becomes part of the mysterious plan of God's salvation, the final outcome of which is the salvation of "all Israel" (Rm 11:26).

The "covenants of promise" are explicitly mentioned in Ep 2:12 to announce that access to them is now open to the "nations," Christ having broken down "the wall of separation," that is to say, the Law which blocked access to them for non-Jews (cf. Ep 2:14–15).

The Pauline Letters, then, manifest a twofold conviction: the insufficiency of the legal covenant of Sinai, on the one hand, and on the other, the validity of the covenant-promise. This latter finds its fulfillment in justification by faith in Christ, offered "to the Jew first, but also to the Greek" (Rm 1:16). Their refusal of faith in Christ places the Jewish people in a situation of disobedience, but they are still "loved" and promised God's mercy (cf. Rm 11:26–32).

42. *The Letter to the Hebrews* quotes *in extenso* the prophetic message of the "new covenant"[139] and proclaims its fulfillment in Christ, "mediator of the new covenant."[140] It demonstrates the insufficiency of the cultic institutions of the "first covenant"; priesthood and sacrifices were incapable of overcoming the obstacle set by sins, and incapable of establishing an authentic mediation between God and his people.[141] Those institutions are now abrogated to make way for the sacrifice and priesthood of Christ (Heb 7:18–19; 10:9). For Christ has overcome all obstacles by his redemptive obedience (Heb 5:8–9; 10:9–10), and has opened access to God for all believers (Heb 4:14–16; 10:19–22). In this way, the covenant announced and prefigured in the Old Testament is fulfilled. It is not simply a renewal of the Sinai covenant, but the establishment of a covenant that is truly new, founded on a new base, Christ's personal sacrificial offering (cf. 9:14–15).

God's "covenant" with David is not mentioned explicitly in the New Testament, but Peter's discourse in Acts links the resurrection of Jesus to the "oath" sworn by God to David (Acts 2:20), an oath called a covenant with David in Ps 89:4 and 132:11. The Pauline discourse in Acts 13:34 makes a

---

139. Heb 8:7–13; Jer 31:31–34 LXX.

140. Heb 9:15; cf. 7:22; 12:24.

141. Heb 7:18; 9:9; 10:1, 4, 11.

similar connection by employing the expression of Is 55:3 ("the holy things guaranteed to David"), which, in the Isaian text, defines an "eternal covenant." The resurrection of Jesus, "son of David,"[142] is thus presented as the fulfillment of the covenant-promise given by God to David.

The conclusion which flows from all these texts is that the early Christians were conscious of being in profound continuity with the covenant plan manifested and realized by the God of Israel in the Old Testament. Israel continues to be in a covenant relationship with God, because the covenant-promise is definitive and cannot be abolished. But the early Christians were also conscious of living in a new phase of that plan, announced by the prophets and inaugurated by the blood of Jesus, "blood of the covenant," because it was shed out of love (cf. Rv 1:5[b]–6).

6. The Law

43. The Hebrew word *Tôrâh,* translated "law," more precisely means "instruction," that is, both teaching and directives. The *Tôrâh* is the highest source of wisdom.[143] The Law occupies a central place in the Jewish Scriptures and in their religious practice from biblical times to our own day. This is why, from apostolic times, the Church had to define itself in relation to the Law, following the example of Jesus himself, who gave it its proper significance by virtue of his authority as Son of God.[144]

---

142. Mt 1:1; 9:27; etc.; cf. Lk 1:32; Rm 1:3.
143. Dt 4:6–8; Si 24:22–27; Ba 3:38—4:4.
144. Mt 5:21–48; Mk 2:23–27.

a) Law in the Old Testament

Israel's Law and cult are developed throughout the Old Testament. The different collections of laws[145] can also serve as guides for the chronology of the Pentateuch.

The gift of the Law. The Law is, first of all, God's gift to his people. The gift of the Law is the subject of a main narrative of composite origin[146] and of complementary narratives,[147] among which 2 Kg 22—23 has a special place because of its importance for the Deuteronomist. Ex 19—24 integrates the Law with the "covenant" *(berît)* which the Lord concludes with Israel on the mountain of God, during a theophany before the whole of Israel (Ex 19—20), and then to Moses himself[148] and to the seventy representatives of Israel (Ex 24:9–11). These theophanies, together with the covenant, signify a special grace for the people, present and future,[149] and the laws revealed at that moment in time are their lasting pledge.

But the narrative traditions also link the gift of the Law with the breaking of the covenant that results from violation of the monotheism prescribed in the Decalogue.[150]

---

145. Decalogue: Ex 20:1–17; Dt 5:6–21; Covenant Code: Ex 20: 22—23:19; the collection of Ex 34; Deuteronomic Law: Dt 12—28; Holiness Code: Lv 17—26; Priestly Laws: Ex 25—31; 35—40; Lv 1—7; 8—10; 11—16, etc.

146. Ex 19—24; 32—34; cf. Dt 5:9–10.

147. Gn 17; Ex 12—13; 15:23–26, etc.

148. Ex 20:19 – 21; Dt 5:23 – 31.

149. Ex 19:5 – 6; 24:10 –11.

150. Ex 32—34; Ex 20:2 – 6 and par.

"The spirit of the Laws" according to the Tôrâh. The laws contain moral precepts (ethical), juridical (legal), ritual and cultural (a rich assemblage of religious and profane customs). They are of a concrete nature, expressed sometimes as absolutes (e.g., the Decalogue), at other times as particular cases that concretize general principles. They then have the status of precedent and serve as analogies for comparable situations, giving rise to the later development of jurisprudence, called *halakah,* the oral law, later called the *Mishna.* Many laws have a symbolic meaning, in the sense that they illustrate concretely invisible values such as equity, social harmony, humanitarianism, etc. Not all laws are to be applied, some are school texts for the formation of future priests, judges and other functionaries; others reflect ideas inspired by the prophetic movement.[151] They were applied in the towns and villages of the country (Covenant Code), then throughout the kingdoms of Judah and Israel, and later in the Jewish community dispersed throughout the world.

From a historical point of view, biblical laws are the result of a long history of religious, moral and juridical traditions. They contain many elements in common with the Ancient Near Eastern civilization. Seen from a literary and theological aspect, they have their source in the God of Israel who has revealed them either directly (the Decalogue according to Dt 5:22), or through Moses as intermediary charged with promulgating them. The Decalogue is really a collection sepa-

---

151. For example, the legislation concerning the freeing of slaves: Ex 21:2; Lv 25:10; Dt 15:12; cf. Is 58:6; 61:1; Jer 34:8–17.

rate from the other laws. Its first appearance[152] describes it as the totality of the conditions necessary to ensure freedom for Israelite families and to protect them from all kinds of oppression, idolatry, immorality and injustice. The exploitation experienced by Israel in Egypt must never be reproduced in Israel itself, in the exploitation of the weak by the strong.

On the other hand, the provisions of the Covenant Code and of Ex 34:14–26 embody a range of human and religious values, and also sketch a communitarian ideal of permanent value.

Since the Law is Israelite and Jewish, it is therefore a specific and determinate one, adopted to a particular historical people. But it has also an exemplary value for the whole of humanity (Dt 4:6). For this reason, it is an eschatological good promised to all the nations because it will serve as an instrument of peace (Is 2:1–4; Mi 4:1–3). It embodies a religious anthropology and an ensemble of values that transcend both the people and the historical conditions of which the biblical laws are in part the product.

Tôrâh spirituality. As a manifestation of the all-wise divine will, the commandments become more and more important in the social and individual life of Israel. The Law becomes omnipresent there, especially from the time of the Exile (6th century). Thus a form of spirituality arose that was marked by a profound veneration for the *Tôrâh.* Its observance was regarded as a necessary expression of the "fear of the Lord" and the perfect form of service of God. The Psalms, Sirach and Baruch are witnesses within the Scriptures themselves. Psalms

152. Ex 20:2; Dt 5:6.

1, 19, and 119, as *Tôrâh* Psalms, enjoy a structural role in the organization of the Psalter. The *Tôrâh* revealed to mankind is also the organizing principle of the created universe. In observing that Law, believing Jews found therein their joy and their blessings, and participated in the universal creative wisdom of God. This wisdom revealed to the Jewish people is superior to the wisdom of the nations (Dt 4:6, 8), in particular to that of the Greeks (Ba 4:1– 4).

b) Law in the New Testament

44. Matthew, Paul, the Letter to the Hebrews and James devote an explicit theological reflection to the significance of the Law after the coming of Jesus Christ.

The Gospel of *Matthew* reflects the situation of the Matthean ecclesial community after the destruction of Jerusalem (70 A.D.). Jesus affirms the permanent validity of the Law (Mt 5:18–19), but in a new interpretation given with full authority (Mt 5:21– 48). Jesus "fulfills" the Law (Mt 5:17) by radicalizing it: at times by abolishing the letter of the Law (divorce, law of the talion), at other times, by giving a more demanding interpretation (murder, adultery, oaths), or a more flexible one (sabbath). Jesus insists on the double commandment of love of God (Dt 6:5) and of neighbor (Lv 19:18), on which "depends all the Law and the Prophets" (Mt 22:34 –40). Along with the Law, Jesus, the new Moses, imparts knowledge of God's will to mankind, to the Jews first of all, then to the nations as well (Mt 28:19– 20).

The *Pauline theology* of the Law is rich, but imperfectly unified. This is due to the nature of the writings and to a process of thinking still being worked out in a theological terrain not yet explored in depth. Paul's reflection on the Law was sparked by his own personal spiritual experience and by his apostolic ministry. By his spiritual experience: after his encounter with Christ (1 Co 15:8), Paul realized that his zeal for the Law had led him astray to the point of leading him to "persecute the Church of God" (15:9; Ph 3:6), and that by adhering to Christ, he was renouncing that zeal (Ph 3:7– 9). Through his apostolic experience: since his ministry concerned non-Jews (Gal 2:7; Rm 1:5), it posed a question: does the Christian faith demand of non-Jews submission to the Jewish Law and, in particular, to the legal observances that are the marks of Jewish identity (circumcision, dietary regulations, calendar)? A positive response would have been disastrous for Paul's apostolate. Wrestling with this problem, he was not content with pastoral considerations: he undertook a deeper doctrinal exploration.

Paul becomes acutely aware that the coming of Christ demands that he redefine the function of the Law. For Christ is the "end of the Law" (Rm 10:4), at once the goal toward which it progressed and the terminal moment where its rule ends, because from now on, it is no longer the Law that will give life—it could not do so effectively anyway[153]—it is faith in Christ that justifies and gives life.[154] The Christ risen from the dead transmits his new life to believers (Rm 6:9–11) and assures them of their salvation (Rm 10:9–10).

Henceforth, what is to be the role of the Law? Paul struggled to give an answer. He is aware of the positive func-

---

153. Rm 7:10; Gal 3:21– 22.
154. Rm 1:17; Gal 2:19 – 20.

tion of the Law: it is one of Israel's privileges (Rm 9:4), "the Law of God" (Rm 7:22); it is summed up in the love of neighbor;[155] it is "holy" and "spiritual" (Rm 7:12, 14). According to Ph 3:6, the Law defines a certain "justice." On the other hand, the Law automatically opens up the possibility of a contrary choice: "If it had not been for the Law, I would not have known sin. I would not have known what it is to covet if the Law had not said 'you shall not covet'" (Rm 7:7). Paul frequently speaks of this option inescapably inherent in the gift of the Law, for example, when he says that in the concrete human condition ("the flesh") "sin" prevents mankind from adhering to the Law (Rm 7:23–25), or that "the letter" of the Law, deprived of the Spirit that enables one to fulfill the Law, ends by bringing death (2 Co 3:6–7).

Contrasting "the letter" and "the spirit," the Apostle sets up a dichotomy as he did in the case of Adam and Christ; he places what Adam (that is, the human being deprived of grace) is capable of doing against what Christ (that is, grace) brings about. Indeed, for pious Jews, the Law was part of God's plan where both the promises and faith also had their place, but Paul wants to speak about what the Law can do by itself, as "letter," that is, by abstracting from providence which always accompanies the human being, unless he wishes to establish his own justice.[156]

If, according to 1 Co 15:56, "the sting of death is sin and the power of sin is the Law," it follows that the Law, insofar as it is letter, kills, albeit indirectly. Consequently, the minis-

---

155. Lv 19:18; Gal 5:14; Rm 13:8–10.
156. Rm 10:3; Ph 3:9.

try of Moses could be called a ministry of death (2 Co 3:7), of condemnation (3:9). Nevertheless, this ministry was surrounded by a glory (splendor coming from God) so that Israelites could not even look on the face of Moses (3:7). This glory loses its luster by the very fact that a superior glory (3:10) now exists, that of the "ministry of the Spirit" (3:8).

45. The Letter to the Galatians declares that "all who rely on the works of the Law are under a curse," for the Law curses "everyone who does not observe and obey all the things written in the book of the Law."[157] The Law is opposed here to the way of faith, proposed elsewhere by the Scriptures;[158] it indicates the way of works, leaving us to our own resources (3:12). Not that the Apostle is opposed to "works." He is only against the human pretension of saving oneself through the "works of the Law." He is not against works of faith—which, elsewhere, often coincide with the Law's content—works made possible by a life-giving union with Christ. On the contrary, he declares that "what matters" is "faith that works through love."[159]

Paul is aware that the coming of Christ has led to a change of regime. Christians no longer live under the Law, but by faith in Christ (Gal 3:24 – 26; 4:3 – 7), which is the regime of grace (Rm 6:14 –15).

As regards the central contents of the Law (the Decalogue and that which is in accordance with its spirit), Gal 5:18 – 23 affirms first of all: "If you are led by the Spirit, you are not

---

157. Gal 3:10, quoting Dt 27:26.
158. Gal 3:11; Hab 2:4.
159. Gal 5:6; cf. 5:13; 6:9 –10.

subject to the Law" (5:18). Having no need of the Law, a person will spontaneously abstain from "works of the flesh" (5:19–21) and will produce "the fruit of the Spirit" (5:22). Paul adds that the Law is not contrary to this (5:23), because believers will fulfill all that the Law demands, and will also avoid what the Law prohibits. According to Rm 8:1–4, "the law of the Spirit of life in Christ Jesus" has freed believers from the powerlessness of the Mosaic Law in such a way that "the just precepts of the Law may be fulfilled." One of the reasons for redemption was precisely to obtain this fulfillment of the Law!

In the *Letter to the Hebrews,* the Law appears as an institution that was useful in its time and place.[160] But true mediation between the sinful people and God is not in its power (7:19; 10:1). Only the mediation of Christ is efficacious (9:11–14). Christ is a High Priest of a new kind (7:11, 15). Because of the connection between Law and priesthood, "the change of priesthood involves a change of law" (7:12). In saying this, the author echoes Paul's teaching according to which Christians are no longer under the Law's regime, but under that of faith in Christ and of grace. For a relationship with God, the author insists, is not through the observance of the Law, but through "faith," "hope" and "love" (10:22, 23, 24).

For *James,* as for the Christian community at large, the moral demands of the Law continue to serve as a guide (2:11), but as interpreted by the Lord. The "royal law" (2:8), that of the "kingdom" (2:5), is the precept of love of neighbor.[161] This

---

160. Heb 2:2; 7:5, 28; 8:4; 9:19, 22; 10:8, 28.
161. Lv 19:18; Jas 2:8; 4:11.

is "the perfect law of liberty" (1:25; 2:12–13), which is concerned with working through a faith that is active (2:14 – 26).

This last example shows the variety of positions in relation to the Law expressed in the New Testament, and their fundamental agreement. James does not announce, like Paul and the Letter to the Hebrews, the end of the Law's reign, but he agrees with Matthew, Mark, Luke and Paul in underlining the priority not only of the Decalogue but also the precept of love of neighbor (Lv 19:18), which leads to the perfect observance of the Decalogue and to surpass it. The New Testament then depends on the Old. It is read in the light of Christ, who has confirmed the precept of love and has given it a new dimension: "Love one another as I have loved you" (Jn 13:34; 15:12), that is, to the sacrifice of one's life. The Law is thereby more than fulfilled.

7. Prayer and cult, Temple and Jerusalem

a) *In the Old Testament*

46. In the Old Testament, prayer and cult occupy an important place because these activities are privileged moments of the personal and communal relationship of the Israelites with God who has chosen and called them to live within his covenant.

Prayer and cult in the Pentateuch. The narratives show typical situations of prayer, especially in Gn 12–50. Cries of distress (32:10–13), requests for favor (24:12–14), acts of thanksgiving (24:48), as well as vows (28:20 – 22) and consultations of the Lord about the future (25:22 – 23) are to be found. During the Exodus, Moses intercedes[162] and the people are saved from extermination (32:10, 14).

As a primary source for the knowledge of the institutions, the Pentateuch assembles etiologies that explain the origin of places, times and sacred institutions—*places* like Shechem, Bethel, Mamre, Beersheba,[163] sacred *times* like the sabbath, sabbatical year, jubilee year. Feast days are fixed, including the Day of Atonement.[164]

The cult is a gift from the Lord. Many texts in the Old Testament insist on this perspective. The revelation of God's name is purely gratuitous (Ex 3:14–15). It is the Lord who makes possible the celebration of sacrifices, because it is he who makes available the blood of animals for this purpose (Lv 17:11). Before becoming the people's offering to God, the firstfruits and the tithes are God's gift to the people (Dt 26:9–10). It is God who institutes priests and Levites and designs the sacred utensils (Ex 25—30).

The collections of the Law (cf. above, n. 43) contain numerous liturgical directives and diverse explanations of the purpose of the cultic order. The fundamental distinctions between pure and impure, on the one hand, and holy and profane, on the other, serve to organize space and time, even to the details of daily life, and consequently social and individual living is regulated. Impurity places the affected per-

---

162. Ex 32:11–13, 30–32, etc.

163. Shechem: Gn 12:6–7; Bethel: 12:8; Mamre: 18:1–15; Beersheba: 26:23–25.

164. Sabbath: Gn 2:1–3; Ex 20:8–11; sabbatical year: Lv 25:2–7, 20–22; jubilee year: 25:8–19; feasts: Ex 23:14–17; Lv 23; Dt 16:1–17; Day of Atonement: Lv 16:23, 27–32.

sons and things outside the socio-cultic space, while what is pure is completely integrated with it. Ritual activity includes multiple purifications to reintegrate the impure into the community.[165] Inside the circle of purity, another limit separates the profane (which is pure) from the holy (which is pure and also reserved to God). The holy (or the sacred) is the domain of God. The liturgy of the "Priestly" (P) source also distinguishes "holy" from "Holy of Holies." Holy places are accessible to priests and Levites, but not to the people ("laity"). Sacred space is always set apart.[166]

Sacred time restricts profane employment (prohibition of work, the sabbath day, sowing and reaping during the sabbatical year). It corresponds to the return of the created order to its original state before it was delivered to mankind.[167]

Space, persons and sacred things must be made holy (consecrated). Consecration removes what is incompatible with God, impurity and sin, which are opposed to the Lord. The cult includes multiple rites of pardon (expiations) to restore holiness,[168] which implies that God is near.[169] The people are consecrated and must be holy (Lv 11:44 – 45). The purpose of the cult is that the people be made holy—through expiation, purification and consecration—and be at the service of God.

The cult is a vast symbolism of grace, an expression of God's "condescension" (in the patristic sense of beneficent

---

165. Note that the Old Testament knows nothing of impure times.
166. Gn 28:16 –18; Ex 3:5; Jos 5:15.
167. Ex 23:11–12; Lv 25:6 –7.
168. Lv 4—5; 16; 17:10 –12; Is 6:5 –7, etc.
169. Ex 25:8 – 9; Dt 4:7, 32 – 34.

adaptation) toward human beings, since he established it for pardon, purification, sanctification and preparation for direct contact with his presence (*kabôd,* glory).

47. *Prayer and cult in the Prophets.* The book of Jeremiah contributes much to the appreciation of prayer. It contains "confessions," dialogues with God, in which the prophet, both as an individual and as a representative of his people, expresses a deep, interior crisis about election and the realization of God's plan.[170] Many prophetic books include psalms and canticles[171] as well as fragments of doxologies.[172]

Among the pre-exilic prophets, we notice one prominent feature—repeated condemnation of liturgical sacrifices[173] and even of prayer itself.[174] The rejection seems radical, but these invectives are not to be interpreted as an abrogation of the cult, or a denial of their divine origin. Their aim is to denounce the contradiction between the conduct of the participants and the holiness of God which they claim to be celebrating.

Prayer and cult in the other Writings. Three poetical books are of immense importance for the spirituality of prayer. First, *Job:* with a sincerity equal to the art, the protagonist expresses all the states of his soul directly to God.[175]

---

170. Jer 11:19 – 20; 12:1 – 4; 15:15 –18; etc. Later 2 Mc 15:14 presents Jeremiah in the nether world as "the friend of his brothers, who prays much for the people."

171. Is 12:1 – 6; 25:1 – 5; 26:7 –19; 37:16 – 20; 38:9 – 20; 42:10 –12; 63:7—64:11; Jon 2:3 –10; Na 1:2 – 8; Hab 3:1 –19.

172. Am 4:13; 5:8 – 9; 9:5 – 6.

173. Is 1:10 –17; Hos 6:6; Am 5:21 – 25; Jer 7:21 – 22.

174. Is 1:15; 59:3.

175. Jb 7:1 – 21; 9:25 –31; 10:1 – 22; 13:20—14:22; etc.

Then there is *Lamentations,* where prayer and complaint are mingled.[176] And, of course, the *Psalms,* which constitute the very heart of the Old Testament. In fact, the impression given is if the Hebrew Bible has retained so few developments on prayer, it is to concentrate all the beams of light on one particular collection. The Psalter is the one irreplaceable key to reading not only the whole life of the Israelite people, but the whole of the Hebrew Bible itself. Elsewhere, the Writings contain little more than vague general principles[177] and some samples of more or less elaborated hymns and prayers.[178]

An attempt can be made to classify the psalms around four central axes that retain a universal value in all times and cultures.

Most of the psalms revolve around the axis of *liberation.* The dramatic sequence appears to be stereotyped, whether rooted in personal or collective experiences. The experience of the need for salvation reflected in biblical prayer covers a wide range of situations. Other prayers revolve around the axis of *wonder.* They foster a sense of wonder, contemplation and praise. The axis of *instruction* gathers up three types of meditative prayer: syntheses of sacred history, instruction for personal and communal moral choices (frequently including prophetic words and messages), description of the conditions necessary for participation in the cult. Finally, some prayers revolve around the axis of *popular feasts.* There

---

176. Lm 1:9 –11, 20 – 22; 2:20; 3:41– 45, 55 – 66; 5:19 –22.

177. Pr 15:8, 29; 28:9.

178. Pr 30:7–9; Dn 2:20 –23; 4:31– 32, 34; 9:4 –19 (cf. vv. 20, 23), and more frequently in the deuterocanonical writings.

are four in particular: harvests, marriages, pilgrimages, and political events.

48. Privileged *places* of prayer include sacred spaces and sanctuaries, especially the Jerusalem Temple. But prayer is always possible in the privacy of one's home. Sacred *times,* fixed by the calendar, mark the times for prayer, even personal prayer, as well as the ritual hours of sacrifice, especially morning and evening. We notice different *postures* for prayer: standing, with raised hands, kneeling, fully prostrate, sitting or lying down.

If one can distinguish between the permanent and the dispensable elements in thought and language, the treasury of Israel's prayer can serve to express, at a profound level, the prayer of human beings in all times and places, that is to say, the *permanent value* of those texts. Certain psalms, however, express a type of prayer that will gradually become obsolete, in particular, the curses and imprecations hurled at enemies.

In appropriating the prayers of the Old Testament just as they are, Christians reread them in light of the paschal mystery, which at the same time gives them an extra dimension.

The Jerusalem Temple. Built by Solomon (c. 950 B.C.), this edifice of stone, dominating the hill of Zion, has enjoyed a central place in Israelite religion. Aided by the religious reform of Josiah (640 – 609),[179] the deuteronomic law prescribed one sanctuary in the land for all the people (Dt 12:2–7). The Jerusalem sanctuary was designated as "the place chosen by the LORD your God as a dwelling for his name" (12:11, 21, etc.).

---

179. 2 Kg 22—23.

Several etiological narratives explain this choice.[180] The priestly theology (P), for its part, designated this presence by the word "glory" *(kabôd),* evoking the manifestation of God, at one and the same time both fascinating and awesome, especially in the Holy of Holies, above the ark of the covenant covered by the propitiatory:[181] the nearest contact with God is based on pardon and grace. That is why the destruction of the Temple (587) was the equivalent of total desolation,[182] and took on the proportions of a national catastrophe. The eagerness to rebuild it at the end of the Exile (Hg 1—2) and to celebrate there a worthy cult (Ml 1—3), became the criterion of the fear of God. The Temple radiated blessing to the ends of the earth (Ps 65). Hence the importance of pilgrimage, as a symbol of unity (Ps 122). In the work of the Chronicler, the Temple is clearly at the center of all religious and national life.

The Temple is both *functional and symbolic space.* It serves as the place of the cult, especially sacrifice, prayer, teaching, healing and royal enthronement. As in all religions, the material edifice here below evokes the mystery of the divine dwelling in heaven above (1 Kg 8:30). Because of the special presence of the living God, the Temple becomes the origin par excellence of life (communal birth, rebirth after sin), and of knowledge (word of God, revelation, wisdom). It plays the role of axis and center of the world. Nevertheless, a critical *relativization* of the *symbolism* of the holy place can

---

180. Gn 14:18–20; 2 Sm 7; 24; Ps 132.

181. Ex 25:10–22; Lv 16:12–15 (and Rm 3:25; Heb 9:5).

182. Mi 3:12; Jer 26:18; etc.

be observed. It can never guarantee and "contain" the divine presence.[183] Parallel to the criticism of a hypocritical and formalist cult, the prophets exposed the conceit of placing unconditional confidence in the holy place (Jer 7:1–15). A symbolic vision solemnly presents "the glory of the Lord" departing from the holy place.[184] But this glory will return to the Temple (Ezk 43:1–9), to an ideal, restored one (40–42), a source of fecundity, healing and salvation (47:1–12). Before this return, God promises the exiles that he himself will be "a sanctuary" (11:16) for them.

Jerusalem. From a theological perspective, the history of the city has its origin in a divine choice (1 Kg 8:16). David conquered Jerusalem, an ancient Canaanite city (2 Sm 5:6–12). He transferred the ark of the covenant there (2 Sm 6—7). Solomon built the Temple there (1 Kg 6). Thus the city ranked among the older sacred places in Judah and Israel where people went on pilgrimage. In the war of Sennacherib against Hezekiah in 701 (2 Kg 18:13), Jerusalem alone among the towns of Judah was spared, although the kingdom of Israel was completely conquered by the Assyrians in 722. The deliverance of Jerusalem had been prophetically announced as an act of divine favor (2 Kg 19:20–34).

Jerusalem is usually designated as "the city chosen by the Lord,"[185] "established" by him (Is 14:32), "city of God" (Ps 87:3), "holy city" (Is 48:2), because the Lord is "in its midst" (Zp 3:17). She is promised a glorious future: assurance

---

183. 1 Kg 8:27; cf. Is 66:1.
184. Ezk 10:3–22; 11:22–24.
185. 1 Kg 8:44, 48; Ze 1:17.

of divine presence "for ever" and "from age to age" (Jl 4:16–21), guaranteed protection (Is 31:4–5) as well as happiness and prosperity. Certain texts even attribute an ideal perfection to this city of cities. Above and beyond its geographical location, she becomes the pole of attraction and the axis of the world.[186]

Nevertheless, the greatness of Jerusalem will not prevent evil descending on the city. Numerous prophetic messages (2 Kg 23:27), symbolic actions (Ezk 4—5) and visions (8—11) announce the rejection and the destruction of the city chosen by God.

Later on, a restored Jerusalem becomes one of the great symbols of eschatological salvation: a city illumined by the Lord,[187] given a "new name" and which becomes again the "espoused" of God.[188] Jerusalem will become paradise regained with the coming of the "new heavens" and the "new earth,"[189] essentially a cultic place (Ezk 40—48), the center of the recreated world (Zc 14:16–17). "All the nations" will assemble there to seek arbitration from the Lord and the divine teaching which will put an end to war.[190]

b) In the New Testament

49. *Prayer and cult.* In contrast to the Old Testament, the New Testament contains no detailed legislation concerning

---

186. Ps 48; 87; 122.
187. Is 60:19–20.
188. Is 54:1–8; 62:2–5.
189. Is 65:17–25; 66:20–23.
190. Is 2:2–4; Mi 4:1–4.

the establishment of cultic institutions and rituals—it briefly prescribes baptism and the celebration of the Eucharist[191]—but it puts a strong emphasis on prayer.

The Gospels frequently show *Jesus at prayer.* His filial love for God, his Father, urged him to give much time to this activity. He rises early to pray, even after a late night due to the influx of the sick people with their maladies (Mk 1:32, 35). Sometimes he spends the whole night in prayer (Lk 6:12). He isolates himself "in desert places" to pray better (Lk 5:16), or ascends "the mountain" (Mt 14:23). Luke shows how intense prayer prepares for or accompanies the more decisive moments of Jesus' ministry: his baptism (Lk 3:21), the choice of the Twelve (6:12), the question of his identity posed to the Twelve (9:18), his transfiguration (9:28), his passion (22:41–45).

The Gospels only rarely report the content of Jesus' prayer. The little they do say shows that his prayer expressed the intimacy with his Father, whom he calls "Abba" (Mk 14:36), a term of familiarity not found in the Judaism of the time, to invoke God. Jesus' prayer is often one of thanksgiving, following the Jewish *berākāh.*[192] During the Last Supper, he "chants the psalms" prescribed by the ritual of the great feast.[193] According to the four Gospels, he quotes eleven distinct psalms.

---

191. Mt 28:19; Mk 16:16; Lk 22:19; Jn 6:53–56; 1 Co 11:24–25.

192. Mt 11:25; Lk 10:21; Mt 14:19 and par.; 15:36 and par.; Jn 11:41; Mt 26:26–27 and par.

193. Mt 26:30; Mk 14:26.

The Son gratefully recognizes that everything comes from his Father's love (Jn 3:35). At the end of the Last Supper Discourse, John puts on the lips of Jesus a long prayer of petition for himself and for his disciples, present and future, thereby revealing how his passion is to be understood (Jn 17). The Synoptics record the suppliant prayer of Jesus at the moment of mortal sadness in Gethsemane (Mt 26:36–44 and par.), a prayer accompanied by a gracious compliance with the Father's will (26:39, 42). On the cross, he makes his own the doleful cry of Ps 22:2,[194] or following Luke, the prayer of abandonment of Ps 31:6 (Lk 23:46).

Alongside the prayer *of* Jesus, the Gospels report many demands and supplications made *to* Jesus, to which he generously responds, underlining at the same time the efficacy of faith.[195] Jesus gave instructions on prayer[196] and through parables encouraged perseverance in prayer.[197] He insisted on the necessity of prayer in times of trial "so as not to come into temptation" (Mt 26:41 and par.).

The example of Jesus gave rise to the disciples' wish to imitate him: "Lord, teach us to pray" (Lk 11:1). He responds by teaching them the *Our Father*. The formulas of the *Our Father*[198] resemble Jewish prayer ("The Eighteen Benedictions"), but with an unparalleled sobriety. In a few words, the *Our Father* offers a complete program of filial prayer: adora-

---

194. Mt 27:46; Mk 15:34.
195. Cf. Mt 9:22 and par; 9:29; 15:28; Mk 10:52; Lk 18:42.
196. Mt 6:5–15; Lk 18:9–14.
197. Lk 11:5–8; 18:1–8.
198. Mt 6:9–13; Lk 11:2–4.

tion (first petition), yearning for eschatological salvation (second petition), compliance with the divine will (third petition), prayer for daily necessities in confident abandon, day after day, to God's providence (fourth petition), request for pardon, conditioned by a willingness to pardon (fifth petition), prayer for deliverance from temptation and mastery of evil (sixth and seventh petitions).

Paul, for his part, gives examples of thanksgiving prayer, expressed in various forms, at the beginning of his letters. He invites Christians to "give thanks in all circumstances" and to "pray without ceasing" (1 Th 5:17).

50. The Acts frequently show *Christians at prayer,* either individually (Acts 9:40; 10:9, etc.) or together (4:24–30; 12:12, etc.), in the Temple (2:46; 3:1), in houses (2:46), and even in prison (16:25). Sometimes prayer is accompanied by fasting (13:3; 14:23). In the New Testament, prayer formulas are usually hymnic: the *Magnificat* (Lk 1:46–55), the *Benedictus* (1:68–79), the *Nunc dimittis* (2:29–32) and numerous passages in the Book of Revelation. They are molded in biblical language. In the Pauline corpus, hymns are Christological,[199] reflecting the Church's liturgy. Like the prayer of Jesus, Christian prayer utilizes the Jewish *berākāh* ("Blessed be God...").[200] In a Hellenistic milieu it was more charismatic (1 Co 14:2,16–18). Prayer is the work of the Spirit of God.[201] Certain things are possible only through prayer (Mk 9:29).

---

199. Ph 2:6–11; Col 1:15–20; 1 Tm 3:16. The hymn in Ep 1:3–14 glorifies the Father for the work accomplished "in Christ."

200. 2 Co 1:3–4; Ep 1:3.

201. Jn 4:23; Rm 8:15, 26.

The New Testament reveals traits of the *early Church's liturgical prayer.* The "Lord's Supper" (1 Co 11:20) occupies a prominent place in the traditions.[202] Its form resembles the liturgy of Jewish festal meals: *berākāh* over the bread at the beginning, over the wine at the end. From the tradition underlying 1 Co 11:23–25 and the Synoptic narratives, the two blessings were brought closer in such a way that the meal was placed, not in between, but either before or after. This rite is a memorial of Christ's passion (1 Co 11:24–25); it creates fellowship *(koinônia:* 1 Co 10:16) between the risen Christ and his disciples. Baptism, a profession of faith,[203] offers pardon for sin, unites with Christ's paschal mystery (Rm 6:3–5) and gives entry into the community of believers (1 Co 12:13).

The liturgical calendar remained that of the Jews (except for the Pauline Christian communities that came from paganism: Gal 4:10; Col 2:16), but the sabbath began to be replaced by the first day of the week (Acts 20:7; 1 Co 16:2) called the "day of the Lord" or the "Lord's day" (Rv 1:10), that is, the day of the risen Lord. Christians continued, at first, to frequent the Temple functions (Acts 3:1), which provided the point of departure for the Christian liturgy of the hours.

The Letter to the Hebrews recognized a certain ritual validity for the ancient sacrificial cult (Heb 9:13), as a prefiguration of Christ's offering (9:18–23). But taking up the criticism expressed in the Prophets and Psalms,[204] it denies all efficacy to

---

202. Mt 26:26–28 and par.; Jn 6:51–58; 1 Co 10:16–17; 11:17–34.

203. Mk 16:16; Mt 28:19–20.

204. Cf. above note 169 and Ps 40:7–9, quoted and commented on in Heb 10:5–10; Ps 50:13–14; 51:18–19.

animal sacrifices for the purification of conscience and for the establishment of a deep relationship with God.[205] The only fully efficacious sacrifice is the personal and existential offering of Christ making him the perfect High Priest, "mediator of the new covenant."[206] In virtue of this offering, Christians can approach God (Heb 10:19–22) through grace and by living a life of self-giving (13:15–16). The Apostle Paul already spoke in this manner (Rm 12:1–2).

51. *The Jerusalem Temple.* During the lifetimes of Jesus and Paul the Temple still existed as a material and liturgical reality. Like all Jews, Jesus went there on pilgrimage; he taught there.[207] He performed a prophetic act there by expelling the merchants (Mt 21:12–13 and par.).

The edifice retained its symbolic role as the privileged divine abode, which represented on earth the dwelling place of God in heaven. In Mt 21:3 Jesus quotes a prophetic word where God himself calls it "my house" (Is 56:7); in Jn 2:16 Jesus calls it "my Father's house." But some texts relativize this symbolism and pave the way for transcending it.[208] As Jeremiah had done, Jesus predicted the destruction of the Temple (Mt 24:2 and par.) and announced, instead, its replacement by a new sanctuary, to be built in three days.[209] After his resurrection, Jesus' disciples will understand that the new Temple was his risen body (Jn 2:22). Paul tells believers

---

205. Heb 9:8–10; 10:1, 11.

206. Heb 5:7–10; 9:11–15; 10:10, 14.

207. Jn 7:14, 28; Mk 12:35; Lk 19:47; 20:1; 21:37; Mt 26:55 and par.

208. Jn 4:20–24; Acts 7:48–49 (in reference to Solomon's Temple, quoting Is 66:1–2), Acts 17:24 (in reference to pagan temples).

209. Jn 2:19; cf. Mt 26:61 and par.

that they are members of this body (1 Co 12:27) and the "temple of God" (3:16–17) or "of the Spirit" (6:19). The First Letter of Peter tells them that united with Christ, the "living stone," they form together a "spiritual house" (1 Pt 2:4–5).

The Book of Revelation frequently speaks of a sanctuary.[210] With the exception of Rv 11:1–2, it is always in reference to "God's heavenly sanctuary" (11:19), from which divine intervention on earth emanates. In the final vision it is said of "the holy city, Jerusalem, which descends from heaven" (21:10), that it has no sanctuary, "for its Temple is the Lord God Almighty and the Lamb" (21:22). This is the final fulfillment of the Temple theme.

Jerusalem. The New Testament fully recognizes the importance of *Jerusalem* in God's plan. Jesus forbids swearing by Jerusalem "because it is the city of the Great King" (Mt 5:35). He resolutely goes up there; it is there that he must fulfill his mission.[211] But he says that the city "did not know the time of its visitation" and he tearfully foresees that this blindness will bring about its ruin,[212] as had already happened in Jeremiah's time.

In the meantime, Jerusalem continues to play an important role. In the Lucan theology, it is at the center of salvation history; it is there that Christ dies and is raised. Everything converges on this center: the Gospel begins (Lk 1:5–25) and ends (24:52–52) there. Then everything begins from there: it is from there that, after the coming of the Holy Spirit, the

---

210. Rv 3:12; 7:15; 11:1–2, 19; 14:15, 17; 15:5, 8; 16:1, 17; 21:22.
211. Mt 20:17–19 and par.; 21:1–10 and par.; Lk 9:31, 51; 13:33.
212. Lk 19:41–44. Cf. Mt 23:37–39; Lk 13:34–35; 21:20–24.

good news of salvation is spread to the four corners of the inhabited world (Acts 8—28). As regards Paul, although his apostolate did not begin from Jerusalem (Gal 1:17), he considers communion with the Jerusalem Church to be indispensable (2:1–2). Elsewhere, he declares that the mother of Christians is "the Jerusalem above" (4:26). The city becomes the symbol of eschatological fulfillment both in future (Rv 21:2–3, 9–11) and in present dimension (Heb 12:22).

Thus, aided by a symbolic intensification already well attested in the Old Testament itself, the Church will always recognize the bonds that intimately unite it to the history of Jerusalem and its Temple, as well as to the prayer and cult of the Jewish people.

8. Divine reproaches and condemnations

a) In the Old Testament

52. The election of Israel and the covenant, as we have seen, resulted in demands for faithfulness and holiness. How did the chosen people respond to these demands? To this, the Old Testament frequently gives an answer that expresses the disappointment of Israel's God, a response full of reproaches and even condemnations.

The narrative writings give a long list of infidelities and resistance to the voice of God, a list beginning with the departure from Egypt. In times of real crisis, which ought to have been occasions for proving their trust in God, the Israelites "murmur,"[213] adopting an attitude of challenge to God's

---

213. Ex 15:24; 16:2; 17:3; etc.

plan and of opposition to Moses, to the point of wanting to "stone" him (Ex 17:4). No sooner was the Sinai covenant concluded (Ex 24) than the people let themselves lapse into the gravest infidelity, idolatry (Ex 32:4 – 6).[214] Faced with this disloyalty, the Lord declares: "I have seen this people, how stiff-necked they are" (Ex 32:9). This pejorative description of them is frequently repeated later[215] and becomes a sort of natural epithet to describe the character of Israel. Another episode is no less important: having arrived at the borders of Canaan and been invited to enter the land which the Lord is giving them, the people refuse to enter, on the grounds that it was too dangerous.[216] The Lord then reproaches his people for their lack of faith (Nm 14:11) and condemns them to wander for forty years in the desert, where all the adults will die (14:29, 34), with the exception of those who unreservedly followed the Lord.

The Old Testament frequently mentions that Israel's disobedience began "from the day their ancestors came out of Egypt," and adds that it has continued "even to this day."[217]

The Deuteronomic history which comprises the books of Joshua, Judges, 1—2 Samuel, and 1—2 Kings, gives an unqualified negative judgment on the history of Israel and Judah between the time of Joshua and the Babylonian Exile. The people and their kings, with few exceptions, have generally

---

214. The golden calf episode is the first narrative episode after the conclusion of the covenant. The intermediate chapters (Ex 25—31) are legislative texts.

215. Ex 33:3, 5; 34:9; Dt 9:6, 13; 31:27; Ba 2:30.

216. Nm 13:31—14:4; Dt 1:20 – 21, 26 – 28.

217. 2 Kg 21:15; Jer 7:25 – 26.

succumbed to the temptation of foreign gods in the religious sphere and to social injustice and every kind of disorder forbidden in the Decalogue. That is why this history ended finally on a negative note, the visible consequences of which were the loss of the promised land with the destruction of the two kingdoms and Jerusalem, including the Temple, in 587.

The prophetic writings contain reproaches that are particularly vehement. One of the principal tasks of the prophets was precisely to "cry out with full voice without holding back" to "announce to my people their rebellion."[218] Among the eighth century prophets, *Amos* denounces the sins of Israel, with primary emphasis on the lack of social justice.[219] For *Hosea,* idolatry is the basic sin, but reproaches extend to many others: "swearing, lying, and murder, and stealing and adultery break out; bloodshed follows bloodshed" (Hos 4:2). For *Isaiah,* God has done all he could for his vineyard, but it has not produced fruit (Is 5:1–7). Like Amos before him (4:4), Isaiah rejects the cult of those who show no concern for justice (Is 1:11–17). *Micah* declares that he is "full of strength to declare to Jacob his crimes" (Mi 3:8).

These crimes led to the greatest threats the prophets could hurl against Israel and Judah: the Lord will reject his people.[220] This will lead to the destruction of Jerusalem and its Temple, where his beneficent and protecting presence dwells.[221]

---

218. Is 58:1; cf. Hos 8:1; Mi 3:8.

219. Am 2:6–7; 4:1; 8:4–6.

220. Rejection of Israel in Hos 1:4–6, 8–9; Am 8:1–2; of Judah in Is 6:10–13; Jer 6:30; 7:29.

221. Mi 3:11–12; Jer 7:14–15.

The last decades of Judah and the beginning of the Exile were accompanied by the preaching of many prophets. Like Hosea, Jeremiah enumerates sins[222] and shows that abandoning the LORD is the root of all evil (2:13); he brands idolatry as adultery and prostitution.[223] Ezekiel does the same in lengthy chapters (Ezk 16; 23) and calls the Israelites a "brood of rebels" (2:5, 6, 7, 8), "stubborn and hard-hearted" (2:4; 3:7). The force of the prophetic accusations is astonishing. What is surprising is that Israel gave them such a large place in its Scriptures, which shows a sincerity and humility that is exemplary.

During the Exile and after, the Judean and Jewish community acknowledged their sins through liturgies and prayers in a national confession.[224]

When they contemplated their past, the people of the Sinai covenant could only pass a severe judgment on themselves: their history had been a long succession of infidelities. The punishments were deserved. The covenant had been broken. But the Lord had never resigned himself to accepting this rupture.[225] He had always offered the grace of conversion and resumption of relations, in a more intimate and stable form.[226]

b) In the New Testament

53. *John the Baptist* follows the ancient prophets in his call for repentance to the "brood of vipers" (Mt 3:7; Lk 3:7) that

---

222. Jer 7:9; 9:1– 8.

223. Jer 3:1–13; 5:7–9.

224. Ezr 9:6 –7, 10, 13, 15: Ne 1:6 –7; 9:16 – 27; Ba 1:15 –22; Dn 3:26 – 45 LXX; 9:5 –11.

225. Hos 11:8 – 9; Jer 31:20.

226. Hos 2:21– 22; Jer 31:31– 34; Ezk 36:24 –28.

flocked to his preaching. This preaching was based on the conviction that a divine intervention was about to take place. The judgment was imminent: "Already the axe is at the root of the tree" (Mt 3:10; Lk 3:9). Conversion was then a matter of urgency.

Like that of John, the *preaching of Jesus* is a call to conversion, made urgent by the proximity of the reign of God (Mt 4:17); it is at the same time the announcement of "the good news," of a favorable intervention of God (Mk 1:14–15). Shocked at their refusal to believe, Jesus had recourse to invective, like the prophets of old. He castigates this "evil and adulterous generation" (Mt 12:39), "unbelieving and perverted generation" (17:17), and announces a judgment more severe than that which befell Sodom (11:24; cf. Is 1:10).

The rejection of Jesus by the leaders of his people, who carried with them the population of Jerusalem, increased their guilt to its extreme degree. The divine sanction will be the same as in Jeremiah's time: the capture of Jerusalem and the destruction of the Temple.[227] But—as in Jeremiah's time—God is not satisfied merely to punish; he also offers pardon. To the Jews of Jerusalem who have "killed the Prince of Life" (Acts 3:15), Peter preaches repentance and promises forgiveness of sins (3:19). Less severe than the ancient prophets, he regards their sin as one committed "in ignorance."[228] Thousands respond to his appeal.[229]

In the *Apostolic Letters,* although exhortations and warnings are very frequent, and accompanied at times by threats of

---

227. Lk 19:43–44; Mt 24:2, 15–18 and par.
228. Acts 3:17; cf. Lk 23:34.
229. Acts 2:41; 4:4.

condemnation for sin,[230] reproaches and condemnations as such are relatively rare, though not lacking in severity.[231]

In the Letter to the Romans, Paul draws up a forceful indictment against "those who by their wickedness suppress the truth" (Rm 1:18). The basic fault of the pagans is their failure to recognize God (1:21); their punishment consists of being handed over by God into the grip of immorality.[232] The Jews are reproached for their inconsistency: their conduct contrasts with their knowledge of the Law (Rm 2:17–24).

Christians themselves are not shielded from reproaches. The Letter to the Galatians contains some very serious ones. The Galatians are accused of turning away from God to follow "another gospel," which is a false one (Gal 1:6); they have "cut themselves off from Christ"; they have "fallen away from grace" (5:4). But Paul hopes for their return (5:10). The Corinthians are reproached for the discord stirred up in the community by the cult of certain personalities,[233] as well as for a serious lapse in charity when they celebrate the "Supper of the Lord" (1 Co 11:17–22). "For this reason," Paul says, "many of you are weak and ill, and some of you have died" (11:30). In addition, the community is severely reprimanded because it has tolerated a case of scandalous misconduct. The offender must be excommunicated, "handed over to Satan."[234] Paul quotes the precept of Dt 17:7: "Drive out the wicked

230. Gal 5:21; Ep 5:5; Heb 10:26–31.

231. 1 Co 4:8; 5:1–5; 6:1–8; 11:17–22; 2 Co 12:20–21; Gal 1:6; 4:9; 5:4, 7.

232. Rm 1:24, 26, 28; cf. Ps 81:13.

233. 1 Co 1:10–13; 3:1–4.

234. 1 Co 5:1–5; cf. also 1 Tm 1:19–20.

person from among you" (1 Co 5:13). The Pastoral Letters take issue with "self-styled teachers of the Law" who have strayed from true charity and sincere faith (1 Tm 1:5–7); their names are given as well as the sanctions imposed on them.[235]

The letters sent "to the seven churches" (Rv 1:11) by the author of the Book of Revelation clearly show the diversity of situations in which the Christian communities lived at the time. Almost all of the letters—five out of seven—begin with praise; two contain praise only, but the other five have reproaches, some of them serious, accompanied by threats of punishment. These reproaches are of a general nature ("you have abandoned your first fervor": 2:4; "you have a name of being alive, but you are dead": 3:1); sometimes they are more precise, as when they are criticized for tolerating "the teaching of the Nicolaitans" (2:15) or for their compromise with idolatry (2:14, 21). All the letters express "what the Spirit is saying to the churches."[236] They show that, in most cases, the Christian communities deserve reproaches and that the Spirit is calling them to conversion.[237]

9. The promises

54. Many of the promises made by God in the Old Testament are reread in the light of Jesus Christ in the New Testament. This poses real and delicate questions which touch upon the dialogue between Jews and Christians; they concern the legitimacy of an interpretation of the promises over and

235. 1 Tm 1:19–20; 2 Tm 2:17–18.
236. Rv 2:7, 11, 17, 29, etc.
237. Rv 2:5, 16, 22; 3:3, 19.

above their original, obvious meaning. Who exactly are the descendants of Abraham? Is the promised land first and foremost a geographical location? What future horizon does the God of Revelation reserve for Israel, the people originally chosen? What becomes of the wait for the kingdom of God? And for the Messiah?

a) Descent from Abraham

In the Old Testament

God promised to Abraham innumerable descendants[238] through the single son, the privileged inheritor, born of Sarah.[239] These descendants will become, like Abraham himself, a source of blessing for all the nations (12:3; 22:18). The promise is renewed to Isaac (24:4, 24) and Jacob (28:14; 32:13).

The experience of oppression in Egypt does not prevent the realization of the promise. On the contrary, the beginning of the Book of Exodus attests many times to the numerical growth of the Hebrews (Ex 1:7, 12, 20). When the people are freed from oppression, the promise is already fulfilled: the Israelites are "numerous as the stars of heaven," but God increases their number even more, as he promised (Dt 1:10–11). The people lapse into idolatry and are threatened with extermination; Moses then intercedes before God on their behalf; he recalls God's oath made to Abraham, Isaac and Jacob to multiply their descendants (Ex 32:13). A grave act of disobedience on the part of the people in the desert (Nm 14:2–4), as at the foot of Sinai (Ex 32), gives rise, as in Ex 32, to

---

238. Gn 13:16; 15:5; 17:5–6.
239. Gn 15:4; 17:19; 21:12.

Moses' intercession, which is answered and saves the people from the consequences of their sin. Nevertheless, the present generation will be excluded from the promised land, with the exception of Caleb's clan which remained faithful (Nm 14:20–24). Subsequent generations of Israelites will enjoy all the promises made to their ancestors on the condition, however, of resolutely choosing "life and blessing" and not "death and curse" (Dt 30:19), which unfortunately the northern Israelites did choose later on, with the result that "the Lord rejected" them (2 Kg 17:20), as he did also the southern kingdom that he subjected to the purifying trial of the Babylonian Exile (Jer 25:11).

The ancient promises were quickly revived for those who returned.[240] After the Exile, to preserve purity of descent, beliefs and observances, "those of Israelite descent separated themselves from all foreigners."[241] Later on, the little Book of Jonah—perhaps also, according to some, Ruth—denounces such closed particularism. This poorly reflects the prophetic message in the Book of Isaiah where God bestows on "all the peoples" the hospitality of his house (Is 56:3 –7).

In the New Testament

55. In the New Testament, the validity of the promise made to Abraham is never called into question. The *Magnificat* and the *Benedictus* refer explicitly to it.[242] Jesus is presented as "son of Abraham" (Mt 1:1). To be a son or daughter of Abraham (Lk 13:16; 19:19) is a great honor. Neverthe-

---

240. Is 61:9; 65:23; 66:22.
241. Ne 9:2; cf. 10:31; 13:3; Ezr 9 —10.
242. Lk 1:55, 73; cf. also Heb 11:11–12.

less, the understanding of the promise differs from the one given in Judaism. The preaching of John the Baptist already relativizes the importance of belonging to the family of Abraham. Descent from him according to the flesh is not enough, nor is it even necessary (Mt 3:9; Lk 3:8). Jesus declares that the pagans "will take their place at the banquet with Abraham," "while the heirs of the kingdom will be cast out" (Mt 8:11–12; Lk 13:28–29).

But it is Paul in particular who develops this theme. To the Galatians, preoccupied with entering, through circumcision, the family of the patriarch, in order to have a right to the promised heritage, Paul shows that circumcision is no longer necessary, for what is important is faith in Christ. By faith, one becomes a son of Abraham (Gal 3:17), for Christ is the privileged descendant (3:16) and, through faith, people are incorporated into Christ and so become "descendants of Abraham, heirs to the promise" (3:29). It is in this way—and not through circumcision—that the pagans will receive the blessing transmitted by Abraham (3:8, 14). In Gal 4:22–31, a daring typological interpretation arrives at the same conclusions.

In the Letter to the Romans (4:1–25), Paul returns to the subject in less polemical terms. He highlights the faith of Abraham, for him the source of justification and the basis of Abraham's paternity which extends to all who believe, whether Jew or pagan. For God had promised Abraham: "You shall be the father of a multitude of nations" (Gn 17:4). Paul sees the promise realized in the many believers of pagan origin who belong to Christ (Rm 4:11, 17–18). He makes a distinction between "children of the flesh" and "children of the promise" (Rm 9:8). The Jews who belong to Christ are both.

Believers of pagan origin are "children of the promise," that is the more important of the two.

In this way, Paul confirms and accentuates the universal import of Abraham's blessing and situates the true posterity of the patriarch in the spiritual order.

b) The promised land

56. Every human group wishes to inhabit territory in a permanent manner. Otherwise, reduced to the status of stranger or refugee, it finds itself tolerated at best, or at worst, exploited and continually oppressed. Israel was freed from slavery in Egypt and received from God the promise of land. Its realization required time and gave rise to many problems throughout the course of its history. For the people of the Bible, even after the return from the Babylonian Exile, the land remained an object of hope: "Those blessed by the LORD" will possess the land (Ps 37:22).

In the Old Testament

The term "promised land" is not found in the Hebrew Bible, which has no word for "promise." The idea is expressed by the future tense of the verb "to give," or by using the verb "to swear": "the land which he swore to give to you" (Ex 13:5; 33:1, etc.).

In the Abraham traditions, the promise of land will be fulfilled through descendants.[243] It concerns the "land of Canaan" (Gn 17:8). God raises up a leader, Moses, to liberate Israel and lead it into the promised land.[244] But the people as a

---

243. Gn 12:7; 13:15; 15:4–7, 18–21; 17:6–8; 28:13–14; 35:11–12.
244. Ex 3:7–8; 6:2–8; Dt 12:9–10.

whole lose faith: of those faithful from the beginning, only a few survive the long journey through the desert; it is the younger generation that will enter the land (Nm 14:26–38). Moses himself dies without being able to enter (Dt 34:1–5). Under the leadership of Joshua, the tribes of Israel are settled in the promised territory.

For the Priestly tradition, the land must as far as possible be without blemish, for God himself dwells there (Nm 35:34). The gift is therefore conditioned by moral purity[245] and by service to the Lord alone, to the exclusion of foreign gods (Jos 24:14–24). On the other hand, God himself is the owner of the land. If the Israelites dwell there, it is as "strangers and sojourners,"[246] like the patriarchs in former times (Gn 23:4; Ex 6:4).

After the reign of Solomon, the heritage land was split into two rival kingdoms. The prophets condemn idolatry and social injustice; they threaten punishment: the loss of the land, conquered by foreigners, and the exile of its population. But they always leave open a way to return to a new occupation of the promised land,[247] while emphasizing also the central role of Jerusalem and its Temple.[248] Later the perspective opens out to an eschatological future. Although occupying a limited geographical space, the promised land will become the focus of attraction for the nations.[249]

The theme of the land should not be allowed to overshadow the manner in which the Book of Joshua recounts the

---

245. Lv 18:24–28; Dt 28:15–68.

246. Lv 25:53; Ps 39:13; 1 Ch 29:15.

247. Am 9:11–15; Mi 5:6–7; Jer 12:15; Ezk 36:24–28.

248. See above II, B, 7, nn. 48 and 51.

249. Is 2:1–4; Mi 4:1–4; Zc 14; Tb 13.

entry to the promised land. Many texts[250] speak of consecrating to God the fruits of victory, called the ban *(chérèm).* To prevent all foreign religious contamination, the ban imposed the obligation of destroying all places and objects of pagan cults (Dt 7:5), as well as all living beings (20:15–18). The same applies when an Israelite town succumbs to idolatry. Dt 13:16–18 prescribes that all its inhabitants be put to death and that the town itself be burned down.

At the time when Deuteronomy was written—as well as the Book of Joshua—the ban was a theoretical postulate, since non-Israelite populations no longer existed in Judah. The ban then could be the result of a projection into the past of later preoccupations. Indeed, Deuteronomy is anxious to reinforce the religious identity of a people exposed to the danger of foreign cults and mixed marriages.[251]

Therefore, to appreciate the ban, three factors must be taken into account in interpretation; theological, moral, and one mainly sociological: the recognition of the land as the inalienable domain of the Lord; the necessity of guarding the people from all temptation which would compromise their fidelity to God; finally, the all too human temptation of mingling with religion the worst forms of resorting to violence.

In the New Testament

57. The New Testament does not develop much further the theme of the promised land. The flight of Jesus and his parents to Egypt and their return to the "land of promise" (Mt 2:20–21) clearly retraces the journey of the ancestors; a

---

250. Jos 6:21; 7:1, 11; 8:26; 11:11–12.
251. Dt 7:3–6; 20:18; cf. Ezr 9:1–4; Ne 13:23–29.

theological typology undergirds this narrative. In Stephen's discourse, which recalls their history, the word "promise" or "promised" is found side by side with "land" and "heritage" (Acts 7:2–7). Although not found in the Old Testament, the expression "land of promise" is found in the New (Heb 11:9), in a passage which, undoubtedly, recalls the historical experience of Abraham to better underline its provisional and incomplete character, and its orientation toward the absolute future of the world and history. For the author, the "land" of Israel is only a symbolic pointer toward a very different land, a "heavenly homeland."[252] One of the beatitudes transforms the geographical and historical meaning[253] into a more open-ended one: "the meek shall possess the land" (Mt 5:5); "the land" is equivalent here to "the kingdom of heaven" (5:3, 10) in an eschatological horizon that is both present and future.

The authors of the New Testament are only deepening a symbolic process already at work in the Old Testament and in intertestamental Judaism. It should not be forgotten, however, that a specific land was promised by God to Israel and received as a heritage; this gift of the land was on condition of fidelity to the covenant (Lv 26; Dt 28).

c) *The eternal and the final salvation of Israel*

In the Old Testament

58. What kind of future awaits the people of the covenant? Down through history the people itself has constantly asked this question in direct connection with the themes of divine judgment and salvation.

---

252. Heb 11:9 –16; see also 3:1, 11—4:11.
253. Ex 23:30; Ps 37:11.

From before the Exile, the prophets questioned the naive hope in a "Day of the Lord" which would automatically bring salvation and victory over the enemy. Quite the contrary, to announce the unhappy lot of a people seriously deficient in social consciousness and faith, they reversed the image of the Day of the Lord into one of "darkness and not light,"[254] not, however, without leaving some little light of hope to glimmer intermittently.[255]

The experience of the Exile, as the result of the breaking of the covenant, posed the same question with maximum urgency: can Israel, far from its land, still hope for salvation from God? Has it any future? First Ezekiel, followed by Second Isaiah, announces in God's name a new Exodus, that is, Israel's return to its own country,[256] an experience of salvation that implies several elements: the gathering together of a dispossessed people (Ezk 36:24) brought about by the Lord himself,[257] a profound interior transformation,[258] national[259] and cultic[260] renewal, as well as the revival of past divine choices, especially the choice of the ancestors Abraham and Jacob[261] and that of King David (Ezk 34:23–24).

More recent prophetic developments continue along the same lines. Prophetic messages solemnly proclaim that the

---

254. Am 5:18–20; 8:9; Zp 1:15.

255. Hos 11:8–11; Am 5:15; Zp 2:3.

256. Ezk 20:33–38; Is 43:1–21; 51:9–11; 52:4–12.

257. Ezk 34:1–31; Is 40:11; 59:20.

258. Is 44:3; Ezk 36:24–28.

259. Ezk 37:1–14.

260. Ezk 43:1–12; 47:1–12.

261. Is 41:8–10; 44:1–2.

race of Israel will endure forever,[262] and will never cease to be a nation before the Lord and will never be rejected by him, despite all that it has done (Jer 31:35–37). The Lord promises to restore his people.[263] The ancient promises made in Israel's favor are confirmed. The post-exilic prophets expand their range within a universal horizon.[264]

Regarding the future, the importance of one particular theme must be emphasized as the counterpart: that of "remnant." Theologically, the future of Israel is guaranteed, but it is a circumscribed group, instead of the whole people, that will be the carrier of national hopes and God's salvation.[265] The post-exilic community considered itself to be this "remnant of survivors," awaiting the salvation of God.[266]

In the New Testament

59. In the light of the resurrection of Jesus, what becomes of Israel, the chosen people? God's pardon is offered to it from the start (Acts 2:38), as well as salvation by faith in the risen Christ (13:38–39); many Jews accepted,[267] including "a multitude of priests" (6:7), but the leaders were opposed to the nascent Church, and in the end, the majority of the people did not attach themselves to Christ. This situation has always aroused serious questions with regard to the fulfillment of the

---

262. Is 66:22; Jer 33:25–26.

263. Is 27:12–13; Jer 30:18–22, etc.

264. Is 66:18–21; Zc 14:16.

265. Is 11:11–16; Jer 31:7; Mi 2:12–13; 4:6–7; 5:6–7; Zp 3:12–13; Zc 8:6–8, etc.

266. Ezr 9:13–15; Ne 1:2–3.

267. Acts 2:41; 4:4; 5:14.

salvific plan of God. The New Testament searched for an explanation in the ancient prophecies and maintained that the situation was foretold there, especially in Is 6:9–10, which is frequently quoted in this regard.[268] Paul in particular experienced great sorrow (Rm 9:1–3) and confronted the problem in depth (Rm 9—11). His "brothers according to the flesh" (Rm 9:3) "have stumbled over the stumbling stone" put there by God; rather than relying on faith, they relied on works (9:32). They have stumbled, but not "so as to fall" (11:11). For "God has not rejected his people" (11:2); witness to that is the existence of a "remnant," who believe in Christ; Paul himself is part of that remnant (11:1, 4–6). For him, the existence of this remnant guarantees the hope of Israel's full restoration (11:12, 15). The failure of the chosen people is part of God's paradoxical plan: it brings about the "salvation of the pagans" (11:11). "A hardening has come upon a part of Israel, until the full number of the Gentiles has come in, then all Israel will be saved" through the mercy of God, who has promised it (11:25–26). Meanwhile, Paul puts Christian converts from paganism on their guard against the pride and self-reliance which lie in wait for them, if they forget that they are only wild branches grafted on to the good olive tree, Israel (11:17–24). The Israelites remain "loved" by God and are promised a bright future, "for the gifts and the call of God are irrevocable" (11:29). This is a very positive doctrine which Christians should never forget.

---

268. Mt 13:14–15 and par.; Jn 12:40; Acts 28:26–27; Rm 11:8.

d) *The reign of God*

60. Many passages in the Bible express the expectation of a completely renewed world through the inauguration of an ideal reign in which God takes and keeps all the initiative. Nevertheless, the two Testaments differ considerably, not only in the importance which each one accords this theme, but especially by the different accents they place on it.

In the Old Testament

The concept of divine kingship has deep roots in the cultures of the ancient Near East. The reign of God over his people Israel appears in the Pentateuch,[269] especially in the Book of Judges (Jg 8:22–23) and in the First Book of Samuel (1 Sm 8:7; 12:12). God is also acclaimed as king of the whole universe, particularly in the royal psalms (Ps 93—99). The Lord reveals himself to the prophet Isaiah (c. 740 B.C., Is 6:3–5). One prophet unveils him as the universal king, surrounded by a celestial court (1 Kg 22:19–22).

During the Exile, the prophets conceive the reign of God as operative in the very heart of the eventful history of the chosen people.[270] So too in more recent prophetic texts.[271] Nevertheless, the theme already begins to take on a more emphatic eschatological coloration,[272] which manifests itself in the sovereign arbitration that the Lord will exercise over the nations of the world from his dwelling place on Mount Zion (Is 2:1–4 = Mi 4:1–4). The greatest degree of escha-

---

269. Ex 15:18; Nm 23:21; Dt 33:5.

270. Is 41:21; 43:15; 52:7; Ezk 20:33.

271. Is 33:22; Mi 2:13; Zp 3:15; Ml 1:14.

272. Is 24:23; Mi 4:7–8; Zc 14:6–9,16–17.

tological concentration is reached in the apocalyptic literature with the emergence of a mysterious figure presented as "one like a son of man," "coming on the clouds of heaven," to whom "was given dominion and glory and kingship" over "all the peoples" (Dn 7:13–14). Here, one is approaching the idea of a transcendent, heavenly, eternal reign, that the people of the saints of the Most High are invited to accept (7:18, 22, 27).

It is in the Psalter that the theme of God's reign reaches its height. There are six psalms in particular.[273] Five have the same key phrase in common: "The Lord reigns," which is placed either at the beginning or in the middle.[274] There is great emphasis on the cosmic, ethical and cultic dimensions of this reign. In Ps 47 and 96 universalism is emphasized: "God reigns over the nations."[275] Ps 99 makes way for human mediation that is royal, priestly and prophetic (99:6–8). Ps 96 and 98 open out to an eschatological and universal reign of God. On the other hand, Ps 114, a Passover psalm, celebrates the LORD both as King of Israel and King of the universe. The reign of God is suggested in many other psalms as well.

In the New Testament

61. The reign of God, a theme well attested in the Old Testament, especially in the Psalter, becomes a major theme in the Synoptic Gospels, because it serves as the basis of Jesus' prophetic preaching, his messianic mission, his death and resurrection. The ancient promise is now fulfilled, in a fruitful tension between the already and the not-yet. Certainly

---

273. Ps 47; 93; 96 —99.

274. At the beginning in Ps 93; 97; 99; in the middle in Ps 47 and 96.

275. Ps 47:9; cf. 96:10.

at the time of Jesus, the Old Testament concept of a "reign of God" that was imminent, terrestrial, political, and centered on "Israel" and in "Jerusalem," was still strongly entrenched (Lk 19:11), even among the disciples (Mt 20:21; Acts 1:6). But the New Testament as a whole brings about a radical change, which was already evident in intertestamental Judaism, where the idea of a heavenly, eternal kingdom makes its appearance *(Jubilees* XV:32; XVI:18).

Matthew most frequently speaks of "the kingdom *of the heavens"* (33 times), a semitism which avoids pronouncing the name of God. It devolves on Jesus to "preach the good news of the kingdom" through teaching, healing of illnesses[276] and the expulsion of demons (12:28). The teaching of Jesus on the "righteousness" necessary for entry into the kingdom (5:20) proposes a very high religious and moral ideal (5:21—7:27). Jesus announces that the reign of God is near at hand (4:17), which inserts an eschatological tension into the present time. From now on the reign belongs to those who are "poor in spirit" (5:3) and to those who are "persecuted for the sake of righteousness" (5:10). Several parables present the reign of God as present and operative in the world, as a seed that grows (13:31–32), as a leaven active in the dough (13:33). For his role in the Church, Peter will receive "the keys of the kingdom of heaven" (16:19). Other parables concentrate on eschatological judgment.[277] The kingdom of God becomes a reality now through the reign of the Son of Man.[278] A com-

---

276. Mt 4:17, 23; 9:35.

277. Mt 13:47–50; 22:1–13; cf. 24:1–13.

278. Mt 16:28; 25:31, 34.

parison between Mt 18:9 and Mk 9:47 shows that the kingdom of God points to the access to the true "life," in other words, the access to the communion that God accomplishes for his people, in justice and holiness through Jesus Christ.

Mark and Luke have the same teaching as Matthew, each with his own nuances. Elsewhere in the New Testament the theme is less prominent, though frequent enough.[279] Without using the expression "kingdom of God,"[280] the Book of Revelation describes the great battle against the forces of evil that produces the establishment of this reign. The "kingship of the world" belongs from now on "to our Lord and his Christ"; "he will reign for ever and ever" (Rv 11:15).

e) The son and successor of David

In the Old Testament

62. In some biblical texts, the hope of a better world is mediated through a human agent. An ideal king is awaited, who will liberate from oppression and establish perfect justice (Ps 72). This waiting takes shape, beginning with the message of the prophet Nathan who promised king David that one of his sons would succeed him and that his kingdom would last forever (2 Sm 7:11–16). The obvious sense of this oracle is not messianic; it did not promise David a privileged successor who would inaugurate the definitive reign of God in a renewed world, but simply an immediate successor who, in turn, would be succeeded by others. Each of David's successors was an "anointed" of the Lord, in Hebrew (*māšîach*), for

---

279. Jn 3:3, 5; Acts 1:3; 8:12, etc; Rm 14:17; 1 Co 4:20, etc.
280. Rv 12:10, "the kingdom of our God."

kings were consecrated by the pouring of oil, but none of them was the Messiah. Other prophecies following Nathan's, in the crises of the succeeding centuries, promised that the dynasty would certainly endure as part of God's fidelity to his people (Is 7:14), but they tended more and more to paint a portrait of an ideal king who would inaugurate the reign of God.[281] Even the failure of the political expectations to materialize only served to deepen that hope. The ancient prophetic messages and the royal psalms (Ps 2; 45; 72; 110) were reread with this hope in mind.

The final results of this revolution appear in the writings from the Second Temple period, and in the writings of Qumran. They express messianic expectation in different forms: royal messianic, priestly, and heavenly.[282] Other Jewish writings combine the expectation of earthly salvation for Jerusalem with an eternal salvation beyond this world, by proposing an earthly and intermediate messianic kingdom that would precede the coming of the definitive reign of God in a new creation.[283] Although messianic hope continued to be part of the traditions of Judaism, it did not appear in all currents as a central and integral theme, even as a special indicator.

In the New Testament

63. For the Christian communities of the first century, however, the promise of an anointed son of David becomes an

---

281. Is 9:1–6; 11:1–9; Jer 23:5–6; Ezk 34:23–24; Mi 5:1–5; Zc 3:8; 9:9–10.

282. 1 QS 9:9–11; 1 QSa 2:11–12; CD 12:23; 19:10; 20:1.

283. 1 Hen 93:3–10; 2 Ba 29—30; 39—40; 72—74; 4 Esd 7:26–36; 12:31–34; Apoc Abr 31:1–2.

essential and basic interpretative key. Although the Old Testament and the intertestamental literature can still speak of an eschatology without a Messiah in the context of the vast movement of eschatological expectation, the New Testament itself clearly recognizes in Jesus of Nazareth the promised Messiah, awaited by Israel (and by the whole of humanity): it is he, therefore, who fulfills the promise. Hence, the concern for emphasizing his Davidic descent,[284] and even his superiority to his royal ancestor, who calls him "Lord" (Mk 12:35–37 and par.).

In the New Testament, the Hebrew term *māšîach* transliterated in Greek as *messias* is only found twice, and is followed by its Greek translation *christos,* which means "anointed."[285] In Jn 1:41 the context points to royal messianism (cf. 1:49: "king of Israel"), in 4:25 to a prophetic Messiah, in accordance with Samaritan beliefs: "He will tell you everything." Jesus here explicitly acknowledges this title (4:26). Elsewhere, the New Testament expresses the idea of Messiah by the word *christos,* but at times also by the expression "he who is to come."[286] The title *christos* is reserved to Jesus except in texts that denounce false messiahs.[287] Together with *Kyrios,* "Lord," it is the most frequently used title to identify who Jesus is. It sums up his mystery. He is the object of many confessions of faith in the New Testament.[288]

---

284. Mt 1:1–17; 2:1–6; Lk 1:32–33; 2:11.

285. Jn 1:41; 4:25.

286. Mt 11:3; Lk 7:19; Jn 11:27.

287. Mt 24:5, 23–24; Mk 13:21–22.

288. Mt 16:16 and par.; Jn 11:27; 20:31; Acts 2:36; 9:22; 17:3; 18:5, 28; 1 Jn 5:1.

In the Synoptics, the recognition of Jesus as Messiah plays a prominent role, especially in Peter's confession (Mk 8:27– 29 and par.). The explicit prohibition against revealing the title, far from being a denial, confirms rather a radically new understanding of it in contrast to a too earthly political expectation on the part of the disciples and the crowds (8:30). The necessary passage through suffering and death is affirmed.[289] Confronted by the high priest during his trial, Jesus clearly identifies himself with the Messiah according to Mk 14:61– 62: the drama of the passion lifts the veil on the specific uniqueness of Jesus' Messiahship, in line with the Suffering Servant who is described by Isaiah. The paschal events open the way to the parousia, in other words, to the coming of "the Son of Man in the clouds of heaven" (Mk 13:26 and par.), a hope already expressed opaquely in the apocalypse of Daniel (Dn 7:13 –14).

In the Fourth Gospel, the messianic identity of Jesus is the object of remarkable confessions of faith,[290] but also the occasion for several controversies with the Jews.[291] Numerous "signs" tend to confirm it. It is plainly a transcendent royalty that is described (18:36–37), incomparably different from the nationalistic and political aspirations current at the time (6:15).

According to Nathan's prophetic message, the son and successor of David will be recognized as son of God.[292] The New Testament proclaims that Jesus is in reality "the Christ,

---

289. Mk 8:31– 37; Lk 24:26.

290. Jn 3:28; 11:27; 20:31.

291. Jn 7:25– 31, 40– 44; 9:22; 10:24; 12:34–35.

292. 2 Sm 7:14; cf. Ps 2:7.

the Son of God,"[293] and gives that sonship a transcendent definition: Jesus is one with the Father.[294]

A privileged witness to the Church's post-paschal faith, Luke's second volume makes the royal consecration (messianic) of Jesus coincide with the moment of his resurrection (Acts 2:36). The demonstration of the title's credibility becomes an essential element of the apostolic preaching.[295] In the Pauline corpus, the word "Christ" abounds, frequently as a proper name, deeply rooted in the theology of the cross (1 Co 1:13; 2:2) and glorification (2 Co 4:4–5). Based on Ps 109 (110), verses 1 and 4, the Letter to the Hebrews demonstrates that Christ is the priest-Messiah (5:5—6:10) as well as royal Messiah (1:8; 8:1). This expresses the priestly dimension of Christ's sufferings and his glorification. In the Book of Revelation, Jesus' Messiahship is set in the Davidic line: Jesus possesses "the key of David" (Rv 3:7); he fulfills the Davidic messianism of Psalm 2[296]; he declares: "I am the shoot and the descendant of David" (Rv 22:16).

For the New Testament then, it is Jesus who fulfills in his person, above all in his paschal mystery, all the promises of salvation associated with the coming of the Messiah. He is Son of David of course, but also Suffering Servant, Son of Man and eternal Son of God. In him, salvation takes on a new dimension. The emphasis changes from a predominantly

---

293. Mt 16:16; Mk 14:61–62 and par.; Jn 10:36; 11:27; 20:31; Rm 1:3–4.

294. Jn 10:30 (cf. 10:24); cf. 1:18.

295. Acts 9:22; 18:5, 28.

296. Ap 2:26–27; 11:18; 12:5; 19:15, 19.

earthly salvation to a transcendent one that surpasses the conditions of temporal existence. It is addressed to every single human being, to the entire human race.[297]

C. Conclusion

64. Christian readers were convinced that their Old Testament hermeneutic, although significantly different from that of Judaism, corresponds nevertheless to a potentiality of meaning that is really present in the texts. Like a "revelation" during the process of photographic development, the person of Jesus and the events concerning him now appear in the Scriptures with a fullness of meaning that could not be hitherto perceived. Such a fullness of meaning establishes a threefold connection between the New Testament and the Old: continuity, discontinuity, and progression.

1. Continuity

In addition to recognizing the authority of the Jewish Scriptures and despite the constant seeking to demonstrate that the "new" events were in conformity with what was predicted (see ch. 1), the New Testament fully appropriates the great themes of the theology of Israel in a threefold reference to past, present and future.

A universal perspective is always present: God is one; it is he who, by his word and spirit, created and sustains the whole universe, including human beings, who are "great" and "noble" despite their "wretchedness."

---

297. Mk 16:15 –16; Jn 4:42.

Other themes are developed in the context of a particular history: God has spoken, he has chosen a people, has freed and saved them innumerable times, has established a covenant relationship with them by the giving of himself (grace) and by offering a way of faithfulness (Law). The person and work of Christ together with the existence of the Church prolong this history.

This opens up for the chosen people wonderful future horizons: posterity (promised to Abraham), living space (a territory), survival beyond crises and testings (due to God's fidelity), and the establishment of an ideal political order (the reign of God, messianism). From the beginning, a reign universal in its scope is envisaged for the blessing given to Abraham. The salvation bestowed by God will spread to the ends of the earth. Indeed, it is Jesus Christ who offers salvation to the entire world.

2. Discontinuity

Nevertheless, it cannot be denied that the passage from one Testament to the other also involves ruptures. These do not submerge continuity. They presuppose it in essentials. Yet these ruptures impinge upon whole tracts of the Law: for example, institutions like the levitical priesthood of the Jerusalem Temple; cultic forms like animal sacrifice; religious and ritual practices like circumcision, rules concerning purity and impurity, dietary prescriptions; imperfect laws such as divorce; restrictive legal interpretations concerning the sabbath. It is clear that—from the viewpoint of Judaism—these are matters of great importance for it. But it is also clear that the radical replacement in the New Testament was already adumbrated in the Old Testament and so constitutes a potentially legitimate reading.

3. Progression

65. Discontinuity on certain points is only the negative side of what is positively called progression. The New Testament attests that Jesus, far from being in opposition to the Israelite Scriptures, revoking them as provisional, brings them instead to fulfillment in his person, in his mission, and especially in his paschal mystery. In fact, none of the great Old Testament themes escapes the new radiation of Christological light.

a) God. The New Testament firmly holds on to the monotheistic faith of Israel: God remains the One[298]; nevertheless, the Son participates in this mystery that from now on will be expressed in a ternary symbolism, already opaquely foreshadowed in the Old Testament.[299] God creates by his word (Gn 1), but this Word pre-exists "with God" and "is God" (Jn 1:1–5), and after entering history through a line of authentic spokespersons (Moses and the prophets), is now incarnate in Jesus of Nazareth.[300] God also creates "by the breath of his mouth" (Ps 33:6). This breath is "the Holy Spirit" sent from the Father by the risen Christ (Acts 2:33).

b) Human beings. The human being is created noble, "in the image of God" (Gn 1:26). But the most perfect "image of the invisible God" is Christ (Col 1:15). And we ourselves are invited to become images of Christ,[301] that is, "a new cre-

---

298. Mk 12:29; 1 Co 8:4; Ep 4:6; 1 Tm 2:5.
299. Ps 33:6; Pr 8:22–31; Si 24:1–23, etc.
300. Jn 1:14–18; Heb 1:1–4.
301. Rm 8:29; 2 Co 3:18.

ation."[302] From our poverty and wretchedness God saves and liberates us through the unique mediation of Jesus Christ, who died for our sins and is risen for our life.[303]

c) *The people.* The New Testament takes for granted that the election of Israel, the people of the covenant, is irrevocable: it preserves intact its prerogatives (Rm 9:4) and its priority status in history, in the offer of salvation (Acts 13:23) and in the Word of God (13:46). But God has also offered to Israel a "new covenant" (Jer 31:31); this is now established through the blood of Jesus.[304] The Church is composed of Israelites who have accepted the new covenant, and of other believers who have joined them. As a people of the new covenant, the Church is conscious of existing only in virtue of belonging to Christ Jesus, the Messiah of Israel, and because of its link with the apostles, who were all Israelites. Far from being a substitution for Israel,[305] the Church is in solidarity with it. To the Christians who have come from the nations, the Apostle Paul declares that they are grafted to the good olive tree which is Israel (Rm 11:16, 17). That is to say, the Church is conscious of being given a universal horizon by Christ, in conformity with Abraham's vocation, whose descendants from now on are multiplied in a filiation founded on faith in Christ (Rm 4:11–12). The reign of God is no longer confined to Israel alone, but is open to all, including the pagans, with a

---

302. 2 Co 5:17; Gal 6:15.

303. Rm 4:25; Ph 3:20–21; 1 Tm 2:5–6; Heb 9:15.

304. Lk 22:20; 1 Co 11:25.

305. The New Testament never calls the Church "the new Israel." In Gal 6:14, "the Israel of God" very likely designates Jews who believe in Christ Jesus.

place of honor for the poor and oppressed.[306] The hope placed in the royal house of David, although defunct for six centuries, becomes the essential key for the reading of history: it is concentrated from now on in Jesus Christ, a humble and distant descendant. Finally, as regards the land of Israel (including the Temple and the holy city), the New Testament extends the process of symbolization already begun in the Old Testament and in intertestamental Judaism.

Accordingly, for Christians, the God of revelation has pronounced his final word with the advent of Jesus Christ and the Church. "Long ago God spoke to our ancestors in many and various ways through the prophets, but in these last days he has spoken to us through his Son" (Heb 1:1–2).

---

306. Lk 14:12–24; 1 Co 1:26–29; Jas 2:5.

III.

the Temple w...
as is clear i...
scripts. ...
Law ex...
by...

The Jews in the N(

66. Having examined the relationship between the New Testament writings and the Jewish Scriptures, we will now consider the various attitudes to the Jews expressed in the New Testament. We will begin by noting the diversity evident then within Judaism itself.

A. Different Viewpoints within Post-exilic Judaism

1. The last centuries before Jesus Christ

"Judaism" is a term designating the period of Israelite history which began in 538 B.C. with the permission from the Persian authorities to reconstruct the Jerusalem Temple. The religion of Judaism, in many respects, inherited the pre-exilic religion of the kingdom of Judah. The Temple was rebuilt: sacrifices were offered; hymns and psalms were chanted; pilgrimage feasts were again celebrated. Judaism took on a particular religious hue after the proclamation of the Law by Ezra (Ne 8:1–12) in the Persian era. Gradually, the synagogue became an important factor in Jewish life. Diverse attitudes to

...re a source of division for Jews until 70 A.D., ...d the Samaritan schism and in the Qumran manu... ...ivisions based on different interpretations of the ...isted after the year 70 just as they did before.

...he Samaritan community was a dissident group, shunned ...y others (Si 50:25–26). It was based on a particular form of the Pentateuch after rejection of the Jerusalem Temple and its priesthood. The Samaritan Temple was built on Mt. Gerizim (Jn 4:9, 20). They had their own priesthood.

The description of three "parties" or schools of thought given by Josephus—Pharisees, Sadducees, and Essenes (Ant. 13:5, 9; §171)—is a simplification that must be interpreted with circumspection. One can be sure that many Jews did not belong to any of the three groups. Furthermore, the differences between them extended beyond the religious.

The origin of the *Sadducees* is probably to be found in the Zadokite priesthood of the Temple. They apparently became a distinct group in Maccabean times because of the closed attitude of one section of the priesthood toward the Hasmonean rulers. The difficulty of precisely identifying them is evident from a study of the period from the Maccabean revolt against the Seleucids, from 167, to the Roman intervention in 63. The Sadducees became more and more identified with the Hellenized aristocracy who held power; one can surmise that they had little in common with the ordinary people.

The origin of the *Essenes,* according to some authors, dates from around 200 B.C. in an atmosphere of Jewish apocalyptic expectations, but most see it as a reaction to the changing attitude to the Temple beginning from 152, when Jonathan, brother of Judas Maccabeus, was anointed high priest. They are the Hasidim or "pious" who took part in the Maccabean revolt (1 Mc 2:42), but later felt betrayed by Jonathan and Simon, brothers of Judas Maccabeus, who accepted appointment as high priests by the Seleucid kings. What we know of the Essenes has been considerably augmented by the discoveries, beginning in 1947, of about 800 scrolls and fragments at Qumran, near the Dead Sea. A majority of scholars are of the opinion that these documents come from a group of Essenes who established themselves on this site. In *The Jewish War,*[307] Josephus gives a lengthy laudatory description of Essene piety and its way of life that, in many ways, resembled a monastic settlement. Disdaining the Temple ruled by priests whom they judged to be unworthy, the Qumran group formed the community of the new covenant. They sought perfection through strict observance of the Law, interpreted by the Teacher of Righteousness. They awaited an imminent messianic appearance, an intervention by God that would destroy all iniquity and punish their enemies.

The *Pharisees* were not a priestly movement. Apparently, the seizure of the high priesthood by the Maccabees did not preoccupy them. Nevertheless, their very name, which implies separation, is probably the result of strong criticism of the Hasmonean descendants of the Maccabees, from whose growing secularized rule they dissociated themselves. To the written Law, the Pharisees added a second Law of Moses, the oral Law. Their interpretation was less strict than the Essenes and more innovative than the conservative Sadducees who

---

307. *War* 2.8.2–13; §119–161.

accepted only the written Law. They also differed from the Sadducees by professing belief in the resurrection of the dead and in angels (Acts 23:8), beliefs that made their appearance during the post-exilic period.

The relations between the different groups were at times severely strained, even to the point of hostility. It is worth keeping in mind that this hostility can put in context, from a religious viewpoint, the enmity that is found in the New Testament. High priests were responsible for much of the violence. There is the case of a high priest, whose name is unknown, who tried to put to death, probably toward the end of the second century B.C., the Teacher of Righteousness in Qumran during the Yom Kippur celebrations. The Qumran writings are full of polemics against the Jerusalem Sadducean hierarchy, wicked priests accused of violating the commandments, and they likewise denigrate the Pharisees. While exalting the Teacher of Righteousness, they accuse another person (an Essene?) of scoffing and lying and persecuting with the sword "all who walk in perfection" (Damascus Document, ms. A, I, 20). These incidents happened before the time of Herod the Great and the Roman rule in Judea, and so before the time of Jesus.

2. The first third of the first century A.D. in Palestine

67. This is the period corresponding to the life of Jesus which had already begun a little earlier, when Jesus was born before the death of Herod the Great in 4 B.C. After his death, the emperor Augustus divided the kingdom between the three sons of Herod: Archelaus (Mt 2:22), Herod Antipas (14:1, etc.), and Philip (16:13; Lk 3:1). The reign of Archelaus

stirred up hostility among his subjects, and Augustus before long put his territory, Judea, under Roman administration.

What was Jesus' attitude toward the three religious "parties" mentioned above? Three questions in particular merit consideration.

Which was the most important religious group during Jesus' public life? Josephus says that the Pharisees were the main party, extremely influential in the towns.[308] It was perhaps for this reason that Jesus is presented more often in conflict with them than with any other group, an indirect acknowledgment of their importance. Furthermore, this party within Judaism survived better than the others and nascent Christianity had to confront it.

What beliefs did the Pharisees hold? The Gospels frequently present the Pharisees as hypocritical and heartless legalists. There was an attempt to refute this by referring to certain rabbinical attitudes attested in the Mishna, which shows that they were neither hypocritical nor strictly legalist. But this argument is not convincing, for a legalist tendency is also present in the Mishna. Furthermore, it is unknown whether these attitudes codified by the Mishna (c. 200) actually correspond to those of the Pharisees of Jesus' time. However, it must be admitted that in all probability, the presentation of the Pharisees in the Gospels was influenced in part by subsequent polemics between Christians and Jews. At the time of Jesus, there were no doubt Pharisees who taught an ethic worthy of approval. But the firsthand direct testimony

308. *War* 2:8.14; §162; *Antiquities* 18:13; §14.

of Paul, a Pharisee "zealous for the traditions of the ancestors," shows the excess to which this zeal of the Pharisees could lead: "I persecuted the Church of God."[309]

Did Jesus belong to any of the three groups? There is no reason to think that Jesus was a Sadducee. He was not a priest. His belief in angels and the resurrection of the body, as well as the eschatological expectation attributed to him in the Gospels, is much closer to the theology of the Essenes and the Pharisees. But the New Testament never mentions the Essenes, and there is no recollection that Jesus belonged to such a specific community. As regards the Pharisees, who are frequently mentioned in the Gospels, their relationship with Jesus is usually one of opposition, because of his position of non-conformance to their observances.[310]

It is much more likely that Jesus did not belong to any of the sects existing within Judaism at the time. He was simply one of the common people. Recent research has attempted to situate him in various contemporary contexts: a charismatic rabbi from Galilee, an itinerant Cynic preacher, and even a revolutionary zealot. He does not fit into any of these categories.

On Jesus' relationship with the Gentiles and their ways of thinking, there has been much speculation, but there is too little information to go on. During this period in Palestine, even in regions where the greater part of the population was Jewish, Hellenistic influence was strong, but not equally felt

---

309. Gal 1:13–14; Ph 3:5–6; cf. Acts 8:3; 9:1–2; 22:3–5; 26:10–11.
310. Mt 9:11, 14 and par.; 12:2, 14 and par.; 12:24; 15:1–2 and par.; 15:12; 16:6 and par.; 22:15 and par.

everywhere. The influence on Jesus of the culture of the Hellenistic towns like Tiberias on the shore of lake Galilee and Sepphoris (6–7 kilometers from Nazareth) is still uncertain, since the Gospels give no indication that Jesus had any contact with these towns. Neither do we have any evidence that Jesus or his closest disciples spoke Greek in any significant measure. In the Synoptic Gospels, Jesus has little contact with Gentiles; he orders his disciples not to preach to them (Mt 10:5); he forbids imitation of their lifestyle (6:7, 32). Some of his sayings reflect a Jewish attitude of superiority toward the Gentiles,[311] but he knows how to distance himself from such attitudes and affirms instead the superiority of many of the Gentiles (Mt 8:10–12).

What was the attitude of Jesus' early disciples to the Jewish religious environment? The Twelve and others would have shared Jesus' Galilean mentality, although the environs of the lake of Galilee where they lived were more cosmopolitan than Nazareth. The Fourth Gospel reports that Jesus drew disciples from John the Baptist (Jn 1:35–41), that he had Judean disciples (19:38), and that he converted one entire Samaritan village (4:39–42). The group of disciples, then, could very well reflect the pluralism that existed in Palestine at that time.

3. The second third of the first century

68. The first period of direct Roman rule in Judea came to an end in 39–40. Herod Agrippa I, friend of the emperor

---

311. Mt 5:47; 15:26 and par.

Caligula (37–41) and of the new emperor Claudius (41–54), became king of all Palestine (41–44). He gained the support of the Jewish religious leaders and gave the appearance of being religious. In Acts 12, Luke attributes a persecution to him, and also the death of James, the brother of John and son of Zebedee. After the death of Agrippa, which Acts 12:20–23 dramatically recounts, a second period of Roman rule began.

It was during this second third of the first century that the disciples of the risen Christ greatly increased in numbers and were organized into "churches" ("assemblies"). It is likely that the structures of certain Jewish groups influenced primitive Church structures. It may be asked whether the Christian "presbyters" or "elders" were modeled on the "elders" of the synagogues, and whether the Christian bishops ("overseers") were modeled on the Qumran "overseers." Does not the designation of the Christian community as "the way" *(hodos)* reflect the spirituality of the Qumran groups, gone into the desert to prepare the way of the Lord? From a theological viewpoint, some have thought that traces of Qumran influence are to be found in the dualism of the Fourth Gospel, expressed in terms of light and darkness, truth and falsehood, in the battle between Jesus, the light of the world, and the powers of darkness (Lk 22:53), and in the battle between the Spirit of Truth and the prince of this world (Jn 16:11). Nevertheless, the presence of common themes does not necessarily imply dependence.

The Roman procurators for the years 44–66 were men devoid of vision, corrupt and dishonest. Their misgovernment gave rise to the "sicarii" (terrorists armed with knives) and "zealots" (zealous for the Law, devoid of pity), and finally provoked a great Jewish revolt against the Romans. The great Roman armies and their best generals fought to quell this revolt. For Christians, a noteworthy event was the death of James, "the brother of the Lord," in the year 62, following a decision of the Sanhedrin convened by the high priest Ananias (Anne) II. This high priest was dismissed by the procurator Albinus for acting illegally. Only two years later, after a great fire ravaged Rome in July 64, the emperor Nero (54 – 68) persecuted the Christians in the capital city. According to a very ancient tradition, the Apostles Peter and Paul were martyred at that time. Generally speaking, the last third of the first century may be called the post-apostolic era.

4. The final third of the first century

69. The Jewish revolt of 66–70 and the destruction of the Jerusalem Temple precipitated a change in the dynamics of the religious groupings. The revolutionaries (sicarii, zealots and others) were exterminated. The Qumran foundation was destroyed in 68. The cessation of Temple sacrifices weakened the power base of the Sadducean leaders who belonged to the priestly families. We do not know to what extent rabbinic Judaism is the successor of the Pharisees. What we do know is that after 70, the rabbinic masters, "the sages of Israel," gradually came to be recognized as leaders of the people. Those who reassembled at Jamnia (Yavneh) on the coast of Palestine were considered by the Roman authorities to be spokespersons for the Jews. From c. 90–110, Gamaliel II, son and grandson of distinguished interpreters of the Law, presided over "the assembly" in Jamnia. When they speak of Judaism, Christian writings from this period were more and more

influenced by this rabbinic Judaism then in the process of formation. In certain areas, conflicts between the synagogue leaders and Jesus' disciples were sharp. This is evident from the expulsion from the synagogue imposed on "whoever confesses Jesus as the Christ" (Jn 9:22) and, on the other hand, in the strong anti-Pharisee polemic of Mt 23, as well as in the reference made from the outside to *"their* synagogues" as places where Jesus' disciples were flogged (Mt 10:17). The *Birkat ha-minim,* a synagogal "blessing" (actually a curse) against non-conformists is often cited. Its dating to 85 is uncertain, and the idea that it was a universal Jewish decree against Christians is almost certainly wrong. But one cannot seriously doubt that at certain times in different places, local synagogues no longer tolerated the presence of Christians, and subjected them to harassment that could even go as far as putting them to death (Jn16:2).[312]

Gradually, probably from the beginning of the second century, a formula of "blessing" denouncing heretics or deviants of different sorts was composed to include Christians, and much later, they were the ones specifically targeted. Everywhere, by the end of the second century, the lines of demarcation and division were sharply drawn between Christians and Jews who did not believe in Jesus. But texts like 1 Th 2:14 and Rm 9—11 demonstrate that the lines of division were already clearly visible before that time.

---

312. In the second century, the story of the martyrdom of Polycarp witnesses to the "habitual" willingness on the part of Jews in Smyrna to cooperate in putting Christians to death: *"Martyrdom of St. Polycarp,"* XIII, 1.

B. Jews in the Gospels and Acts of the Apostles

70. The Gospels and Acts have a basic outlook on Jews that is extremely positive because they recognize that the Jews are a people chosen by God for the fulfillment of his plan of salvation. This divine choice finds its highest confirmation in the person of Jesus, son of a Jewish mother, born to be the Savior of his people, one who fulfills his mission by announcing the Good News to his people and by performing works of healing and liberation that culminate in his passion and resurrection. The attachment to Jesus of a great number of Jews, during his public life and after his resurrection, confirms this perspective, as does Jesus' choice of twelve Jews to share in his mission and continue his work.

The Good News, accepted wholeheartedly in the beginning by many Jews, met with opposition from the leaders, who were eventually followed by the greater part of the people. The result was that between Jewish and Christian communities a conflict situation arose that clearly left its mark on the redaction of the Gospels and Acts.

1. The Gospel according to Matthew

The relationship between the first Gospel and the Jewish world is extremely close. Many details in it show a great familiarity with the Scriptures, the traditions and the mentality of the Jewish milieu. More than Mark and Luke, Matthew stresses the Jewish origin of Jesus: the genealogy presents him as "son of David, son of Abraham" (Mt 1:1) and goes no further back. The etymology of Jesus' name is underlined: the child of Mary will bear this name "because it is he who will save his people from their sins" (1:21). Jesus' mission during his public life is limited "to the lost sheep of the house of Israel" (15:24), and he assigns the same limits to the mission of the Twelve (10:5 – 6). More than the other evangelists, Matthew often takes care to note that events in Jesus' life happened "so that what had been spoken through the prophets might be fulfilled" (2:23). Jesus himself makes it clear that he has come not to abolish the Law, but to fulfill it (5:17).

Nevertheless, it is clear that the Christian communities kept their distance from the Jewish communities that did not believe in Jesus Christ. A significant detail: Matthew does not say that Jesus taught "in *the* synagogues," but "in *their* synagogues" (4:23; 9:35; 13:54), in this way noting the separation. Matthew introduces two of the three Jewish parties described by the historian Josephus, the Pharisees and the Sadducees, but always in a context of opposition to Jesus. This is also true for the scribes,[313] who are frequently associated with the Pharisees. Another significant fact: it is in the first prediction of the passion (16:21) that the three divisions of the Sanhedrin, "the elders, chief priests and scribes," make their first appearance together in the Gospel. They are also set in a situation of radical opposition to Jesus.

Jesus many times confronts the opposition of the scribes and Pharisees, and finally responds by a vigorous counter-offensive (23:2–7,13 – 36) where the phrase "scribes and Pharisees, hypocrites!" occurs six times. This invective certainly

---

313. This observation is valid for the plural, not for the singular, in 8:19 and 13:52.

reflects, in part at least, the situation of Matthew's community. The redactional context is that of two groups living in close contact with one another: Jewish Christians, convinced that they belong to authentic Judaism, and those Jews who do not believe in Christ Jesus, considered by Christians to be unfaithful to their Jewish vocation in their docility to blind and hypocritical guides.

It should be noted that Matthew's polemic does not include Jews in general. These are not named apart from the expression "the King of the Jews," applied to Jesus (2:2; 27:11, 29, 37) and in the final chapter (28:15), a phrase of minor importance. The polemic is for the most part internal, between two groups belonging to Judaism. On the other hand, only the leaders are in view. Although in Isaiah's message the whole vine is reprimanded (Is 5:1–7), in Matthew's parable it is only the tenants who are accused (Mt 21:33–41). The invective and the accusations hurled at the scribes and Pharisees are similar to those found in the prophets, and correspond to a contemporary literary genre which was common in Judaism (for example, Qumran) and also in Hellenism. Moreover, they put Christians themselves on guard against attitudes incompatible with the Gospel (23:8–12).

Furthermore, the anti-Pharisee virulence of Mt 23 must be seen in the context of the apocalyptic discourse of Mt 24—25. Apocalyptic language is employed in times of persecution to strengthen the capacity for resistance on the part of the persecuted minority, and to reinforce their hopes of a liberating divine intervention. Seen in this perspective, the vigor of the polemic is less astonishing.

Nevertheless, it must be recognized that Matthew does not always confine his polemics to the leading class. The diatribe of Mt 23 against the scribes and Pharisees is followed by an apostrophe addressed to Jerusalem. It is the whole city that is accused of "killing the prophets" and of "stoning those sent to it" (23:37), and it is for the whole city that punishment is predicted (23:38). Of its magnificent Temple "there will not remain a stone upon a stone" (24:2). Here is a situation parallel to Jeremiah's time (Jer 7:26). The prophet announced the destruction of the Temple and the ruin of the city (26:6,11). Jerusalem is about to become "a curse for all the nations of the earth" (26:6), exactly the opposite of the blessing promised to Abraham and his descendants (Gn 12:3; 22:18).

71. At the time of the Gospel's redaction, the greater part of the Jewish population had followed their leaders in their refusal to believe in Christ Jesus. Jewish Christians were only a minority. The evangelist, therefore, foresees that Jesus' threats were about to be fulfilled. These threats were not directed at Jews as Jews, but only insofar as they were in solidarity with their leaders in their lack of docility to God. Matthew expresses this solidarity in the passion narrative when he reports that at the instigation of the chief priests and elders, "the crowd" demands of Pilate that Jesus be crucified (Mt 27:20–23). In response to the Roman governor's denial of responsibility, "all the people" present took responsibility themselves for putting Jesus to death (27:24–25). On the people's side, adopting this position certainly showed their conviction that Jesus merited death, but to the evangelist, such conviction was unjustifiable: the blood of Jesus was "innocent blood" (27:4), as even Judas recognized. Jesus would

have made his own the words of Jeremiah: "Know for certain that if you put me to death, you will be bringing innocent blood upon yourselves and upon this city and its inhabitants" (Jer 26:15). From an Old Testament perspective, the sins of the leaders inevitably bring disastrous consequences for the whole community. If the Gospel was redacted after 70 A.D., the evangelist knew that, like Jeremiah's prediction, Jesus' prediction had also been fulfilled. But he did not see this fulfillment as final, for all the Scriptures attest that after the divine sanction God always opens up a positive perspective. [314] The discourse of Mt 23 does end on a positive note. A day will come when Jerusalem will say: "Blessed is he who comes in the name of the Lord" (23:39). Jesus' passion itself opens up the most positive perspective of all, for, from his "innocent blood" criminally shed, Jesus has constituted a "blood of the covenant," "poured out for the remission of sins" (26:38).

Like the people's cry in the passion narrative (27:25), the ending of the parable of the tenants seems to indicate that, at the time of the Gospel's composition, the majority of the Jews had followed their leaders in their refusal to believe in Jesus. Indeed, having predicted that "the kingdom of God will be taken away from you," Jesus did not add that the kingdom would be given "to other leaders," but would be given "to a *nation* producing its fruits" (21:43). The expression "a nation" is implicitly opposed to the "people of Israel"; this assuredly suggests that a great number of the subjects will not be of Jewish origin. The presence of Jews is in no way ex-

---

314. Is 8:23—9:6; Jer 31–32; Ezk 36:16 – 38.

cluded, for the Gospel community is aware that this "nation" will be set up under the authority of the Twelve, in particular of Peter, and the Twelve are Jews. With these and other Jews "many will come from east and west and will eat with Abraham and Isaac and Jacob in the kingdom of heaven, while the heirs of the kingdom will be thrown into outer darkness" (8:11–12). This universal outlook is definitively confirmed at the end of the Gospel, for the risen Jesus commands the "eleven disciples" to go and teach "all the nations" (28:19). This ending, at the same time, confirms the vocation of Israel, for Jesus is a son of Israel and in him the prophecy of Daniel concerning Israel's role in history is fulfilled. The words of the risen One: "All authority in heaven and on earth has been given to me,"[315] make explicit in what sense the universal vision of Daniel and the other prophets are henceforth to be understood.

Conclusion. More than the other Synoptic Gospels, Matthew is the Gospel of fulfillment—Jesus has not come to abolish, but to fulfill—for it insists more on the continuity with the Old Testament, basic for the idea of fulfillment. It is this aspect that makes possible the establishment of fraternal bonds between Christians and Jews. But on the other hand, the Gospel of Matthew reflects a situation of tension and even opposition between the two communities. In it Jesus foresees that his disciples will be flogged in the synagogues and pursued from town to town (23:34). Matthew therefore is concerned to provide for the Christians' defense. Since that

---

315. Mt 28:18; cf. Dn 7:14, 18, 27.

situation has radically changed, Matthew's polemic need no longer interfere with relations between Christians and Jews, and the aspect of continuity, can and ought to prevail. It is equally necessary to say this in relation to the destruction of the city and the Temple. This downfall is an event of the past which henceforth ought to evoke only deep compassion. Christians must be absolutely on their guard against extending responsibility for it to subsequent generations of Jews, and they must remind themselves that after a divine sanction, God never fails to open up positive new perspectives.

2. The Gospel according to Mark

72. Mark's Gospel is a message of salvation that does not inform us as to who the recipients are. The ending which has been added addresses it boldly "to the whole of creation," "into the whole world" (16:15), an address which corresponds to its universalist openness. As regards the Jewish people, Mark, himself a Jew, does not pass any judgment on them. The negative judgment of Isaiah (29:13) is applied in Mark only to the Pharisees and scribes (Mk 7:5–7). Apart from the title "King of the Jews," which is applied to Jesus five times in the passion narrative,[316] the title "Jew" appears only once in the Gospel, in the course of explaining Jewish customs (7:3), addressed obviously to non-Jews. This explanation comes in an episode in which Jesus criticizes the Pharisees' extreme attachment to "the tradition of the elders," causing them to neglect "the commandments of God" (7:8). Mark mentions

---

316. Mk 15:2, 9, 12, 18, 26.

"Israel" only twice,[317] and twice also "the people."[318] In contrast, he frequently mentions "the crowd," for the most part certainly composed of Jews, and favorably disposed toward Jesus,[319] except in one passion episode, where the chief priests pressure them to choose Barabbas (15:11).

It is toward the religious and political authorities that Mark takes a critical stance. His criticism is essentially of their lack of openness to the salvific mission of Jesus: the scribes accuse Jesus of blasphemy, because he uses his power to forgive sins (2:7–10); they do not accept that Jesus "eats with publicans and sinners" (2:15–16); they say he is possessed by a devil (3:22). Jesus has continually to face opposition from them and from the Pharisees.[320]

The political authorities are less frequently called in question: Herod for the death of John the Baptist (6:17–28) and for his "leaven," juxtaposed with that of the Pharisees (8:15), the Jewish Sanhedrin, a political-religious authority (14:55; 15:1), and Pilate (15:15) for their role in the passion.

In the *passion narrative,* the second Gospel attempts to reply to two questions: By whom is Jesus condemned and why is he put to death? It begins by giving a general answer that puts events in a divine light: all this happened "so that the Scriptures might be fulfilled" (14:49). It then reveals the role of the Jewish authorities and that of the Roman governor.

---

317. Mk 12:29; 15:32.

318. Mk 7:6: 14:2.

319. Mk 11:18; 12:12; 14:2.

320. See also Mk 8:11–12, 15; 10:2–12; 11:27–33.

Jesus was arrested on the orders of the three components of the Sanhedrin, "chief priests, scribes and elders" (14:43). The arrest was the end result of a long process, set in motion in Mk 3:6, where, however, the protagonists are different: there they are the Pharisees who have joined the Herodians to plot against Jesus. A significant fact: it is in the first prediction of the passion that "the elders, chief priests and scribes" appear together for the first time (8:31). In 11:18 "the chief priests and the scribes" search for a way to eliminate Jesus. The three categories meet in 11:27, to put Jesus through an interrogation. Jesus recounts for them the parable of the murderous tenants; their reaction is "to look for a way to arrest him" (12:12). In 14:1, their intention is to apprehend him and "to put him to death." The betrayal of Jesus offers them a suitable opportunity (14:10–11). The arrest, followed by condemnation and death, is therefore the work of the nation's ruling class at that time. Mark regularly opposes the attitude of the leaders to that of "the crowd" or "the people," who are favorably disposed to Jesus. Three times the evangelist notes that in their attempts[321] to have Jesus killed, the authorities were inhibited by fear of the people's reaction. Nevertheless, at the end of the trial before Pilate, the chief priests succeeded in sufficiently inciting the attendant crowd to make them choose Barabbas (15:11) in preference to Jesus (15:13). The final decision of Pilate, powerless to calm the crowd, is to "satisfy" them, which, for Jesus, means crucifixion (15:15).

---

321. Mk 11:18; 12:12; 14:2.

This merely incidental crowd certainly cannot be confused with the Jewish people of that time, and even less with the Jews of every age. It should be said that they represent rather the sinful world (Mk 14:41) of which we are all a part.

It is the Sanhedrin that Mark holds guilty of having "condemned" Jesus (10:33; 14:64). About Pilate, Mark declines to say he condemned Jesus, but that, having no reason to accuse him (15:14), he handed him over to be put to death (15:15), something that makes Pilate even more culpable. The reason for the Sanhedrin's condemnation is that Jesus had uttered a "blasphemy" in his affirmative and circumstantial response to the high priest's question whether he was "the Christ, the Son of the Blessed One" (14:61–64). In this way Mark reveals the most dramatic point of rupture between the Jewish authorities and the person of Christ, a matter that continues to be the most serious point of division between Judaism and Christianity. For Christians, Jesus' response is not blasphemy, but the very truth manifested as such by his resurrection. To the Jewish community, Christians are wrong to affirm the divine sonship of Christ in a way that gives grave offense to God. However painful it be, this fundamental disagreement must not degenerate into mutual hostility, or allow the existence of a rich common patrimony to be forgotten, a heritage which includes faith in the one God.

Conclusion. Any interpretation of Mark's Gospel that attempts to pin responsibility for Jesus' death on the Jewish people is erroneous. Such an interpretation, which has had disastrous consequences throughout history, does not correspond at all to the evangelist's perspective, which, as we have said, repeatedly opposes the attitude of the people or the crowd to that of the authorities hostile to Jesus. Furthermore, it is forgotten that the disciples were also part of the Jewish people. It is a question then of an improper transfer of responsibility, of the sort that is often encountered in human history.[322]

Rather, it is well to recall that the passion of Jesus is part of God's mysterious plan, a plan of salvation, for Jesus came "to serve and to give his life as a ransom for many" (10:45), and has made of the blood that he shed a "blood of the covenant" (14:24).

3. The Gospel according to Luke and the Acts of the Apostles

73. Addressed to the "most excellent Theophilus" to complete his Christian instruction (Lk 1:3–4; Acts 1:1), the Gospel of Luke and the book of Acts are writings very open to universalism and, at the same time, very well disposed toward Israel.

The names "Israel," "the Jews," "the people"

The positive attitude to "Israel" is seen immediately in the infancy narratives, where the name appears seven times. It is found only five times in the rest of the Gospel, in much less positive contexts. The name of the Jews appears only five times, three of which occur in the title "King of the Jews" given to Jesus in the passion narrative. More significant is the use of the word "people," which occurs thirty-six times in the

---

322. This tendency continues to manifest itself: the responsibility of the Nazis has been extended to include all Germans, that of certain western lobbies to include all Europeans, that of certain illegal immigrants to include all Africans.

Gospel (as against twice in Mark's Gospel), usually in a favorable light, even at the end of the passion narrative.[323]

In Acts, there is a positive outlook from the beginning, because the apostles announce the resurrection of Christ and the forgiveness of sins for "the whole house of Israel" (2:36), and they attract numerous followers (2:41; 4:4). The name Israel occurs fourteen times in the first part of Acts (Acts 1:6—13:24), and a fifteenth time at the end (28:20). With forty-eight occurrences, the word "people" is much more frequent; "the people" are well disposed at first to the Christian community (2:47; 5:26), in the end they follow the example of their leaders and turn hostile toward it (12:4, 11), to the extent of seeking the death of Paul, in particular (21:30–31). Paul insists on saying that he "has done nothing against the people" (28:17). The same evolution is reflected in the use of the word "Jews" (79 times). On the day of Pentecost (2:5), the Jews whom Peter addresses and respectfully calls by that name (2:14) are summoned to faith in the risen Christ and adhere to him in great numbers. At the start, the Word is addressed exclusively to them (11:19). But very quickly, especially after Stephen's martyrdom, they become persecutors. The putting to death of James by Herod Antipas was an event that pleased them (12:2–3), and their "anticipation" was that

---

323. Luke notes that "a great multitude of people" followed Jesus (23:27), of whom the greater part were women "who beat their breasts and wailed for him" (23:27). After the crucifixion, "the *people* stood watching" (23:35); this watching prepares them for conversion: at the end when "all the people who had gathered to witness this sight and saw what took place, they beat their breasts and went away" (23:48).

the same fate could be waiting for Peter (12:11). Before his conversion, Paul was a relentless persecutor (8:3; cf. Gal 1:13), but after conversion, from persecutor he became the persecuted: already at Damascus "the Jews plotted to kill him" (9:23). Nevertheless, Paul continues to preach Christ "in the synagogues of the Jews" (13:5; 14:1) and brings to the faith "a great multitude of Jews and Greeks" (14:1), but this success provokes the hostile reaction of the "unbelieving Jews" (14:2). The same treatment is frequently repeated in various ways right up to Paul's arrest in Jerusalem, incited by "the Jews of the province of Asia" (21:27). But Paul continues to proclaim with pride: "I am a Jew" (22:3). He suffers the hostility of the Jews, but does not reciprocate.

The Gospel narrative

74. The infancy narrative creates an atmosphere very favorably disposed to the Jewish people. The announcements of extraordinary births reveal "Israel" (1:68) and "Jerusalem" (2:38) as beneficiaries of salvation in fulfillment of an economy rooted in the people's history. The result is "a great joy for all the people" (2:10), "redemption" (1:68–69), "salvation" (2:30–31), "glory for your people" (2:32). This good news is well received. But a future negative reaction to God's gift is glimpsed, for Simeon predicts to Mary that her Son will become a "sign of contradiction" and foretells that "a fall" will precede "the rising up" (or the resurrection) "of many in Israel" (2:34). Thus he opens up a deep perspective in which the Savior is at grips with hostile forces. A touch of universalism, inspired by Second Isaiah (42:6; 49:6), joins the "light of revelation to the nations" to the "glory of your people Israel"

(2:32), a conjoining which clearly shows that universalism does not mean being anti-Jewish.

In the rest of the Gospel, Luke inserts further touches of universalism: first in relation to the preaching of John the Baptist (3:6; cf. Is 40:5), and then by tracing the genealogy of Jesus back to Adam (3:38). However, the first episode of Jesus' ministry at Nazareth at once shows that universalism will create problems. Jesus appeals to his fellow townspeople to renounce a possessive attitude to his miracles and accept that these gifts are also for the benefit of foreigners (4:23–27). Their resentful reaction is violent; rejection and attempted murder (4:28–29). Thus Luke clarifies in advance what the repeated reaction of Jews will be to Paul's success among the Gentiles. The Jews violently oppose a preaching that sweeps away their privileges as the chosen people.[324] Instead of opening out to the universalism of Second Isaiah, they follow Baruch's counsel not to share their privileges with strangers (Ba 4:3). Other Jews resist that temptation and generously give themselves to the service of evangelization (Acts 18:24–26).

Luke reports gospel traditions depicting Jesus in conflict with the scribes and Pharisees (Lk 5:17—6:11). In 6:11, however, he plays down the hostility of those adversaries by not attributing to them a murderous intention from the beginning, unlike Mk 3:6. Luke's polemical discourse against the Pharisees (11:42–44), later extended to include the "lawyers" (11:46–52), is considerably shorter than Mt 23:2–39. The parable of the Good Samaritan is an instruction on the universal-

---

324. Acts 13:44–45, 50; 14:2–6; 17:4–7, 13; 18:5–6.

ity of love in reply to a lawyer's question (Lk 10:29, 36–37). This puts the Jewish priest and Levite in a bad light, while proposing a Samaritan as a model (cf. also 17:12–19). The parables of mercy (15:4–32), addressed to the Pharisees and scribes, also urge an openness of heart. The parable of the merciful father (15:11–32), who invites the elder son to open his heart to the prodigal, does not directly apply to relations between Jews and Gentiles, although this application is often made (the elder son represents observant Jews who are less open to accepting pagans whom they consider to be sinners). Luke's larger context, nevertheless, makes this application possible because of his insistence on universalism.

The parable of the coins (19:11–27) has some very significant special features. There is the pretender to royalty who suffers hostility from his fellow citizens. He must go to a foreign country to be invested with royal power. On his return, he has his opponents executed. This parable, together with that of the murderous vineyard tenants (20:9–19), is a warning by Jesus of the consequences of rejecting him. Other passages in Luke's Gospel expressing Jesus' pain at the prospect of these tragic consequences complete the picture: he weeps over Jerusalem (19:41–44) and he disregards his own sufferings to concentrate on the misfortune of the women and children of that city (23:28–31).

Luke's passion narrative is not particularly severe on the Jewish authorities. During Jesus' appearance before "the assembly of the elders of the people, chief priests and scribes" (22:66–71), Luke spares Jesus from confrontation with the high priest, the accusation of blasphemy and condemnation, all of which serve to play down the culpability of Jesus' enemies. They bring accusations of a political order before Pilate (23:2). Pilate declares three times that Jesus is innocent (23:4, 14, 22), but intends to "give him a lesson" (23:16, 22) by having him flogged, and finally succumbs to the growing pressure of the mob (23:23–25) that includes "chief priests, leaders of the people" (23:13). In the events that follow, the "leaders" remain hostile (23:35), while the people are more favorably disposed toward Jesus (23:27, 45, 48), just as they were during his public life, as we have already noted. Jesus prays for his executioners whom he generously excuses, "for they do not know what they are doing" (23:34).

In the name of the *risen* Jesus, "repentance and forgiveness of sins" is to be "proclaimed to all the nations" (24:47). This universalism has no polemical connotation, for the phrase emphasizes that this preaching must "begin from Jerusalem." The perspective corresponds to Simeon's vision of messianic salvation, prepared by God as "a light of revelation to the Gentiles and for glory to your people Israel" (2:30–32).

Therefore, what the third Gospel transmits to Acts is then substantially favorable to the Jewish people. The forces of evil have had their "hour." "Chief priests, captains of the Temple guard and elders" have been their instruments (22:52–53). But they have not prevailed. God's plan is fulfilled in accordance with the Scriptures (24:25–27, 44–47), and it is a merciful plan for the salvation of all.

The Acts of the Apostles

75. The beginning of Acts depicts Christ's apostles passing from a narrow perspective, the establishment of the kingdom for Israel (Acts 1:6), to a universal one of witness "to the

ends of the earth" (1:8). The Pentecost episode, curiously enough, sympathetically places Jews in this universal perspective: "There were devout Jews from every nation under heaven living in Jerusalem" (2:5). These Jews are the first recipients of the apostolic preaching, symbolizing at the same time the universal destination of the Gospel. Luke suggests as well, more than once, that far from being mutually exclusive, Judaism and universalism go together.

The kerygmatic or missionary discourses preach the mystery of Jesus by emphasizing the strong contrast between the human cruelty which put Jesus to death and the liberating intervention of God who raised him up. "Israel's" sin was to have "put to death the Prince of Life" (3:15). This sin, which is principally that of the "leaders of the people" (4:8–10) or the "Sanhedrin" (5:27, 30), is recalled only as a basis for an appeal to conversion and faith. Besides, Peter attenuates the culpability, not only of the "Israelites" but even of their "leaders," by saying that they acted "out of ignorance" (3:17). Such forbearance is impressive. It corresponds to the teaching and attitude of Jesus (Lk 6:36–37; 23:34).

Nevertheless, the Christian preaching quickly stirs up opposition on the part of the Jewish authorities. The Sadducees oppose the apostles' "proclaiming that in Jesus there is the resurrection of the dead" (Acts 4:2) in which they do not believe (Lk 20:27). But a very influential Pharisee, Gamaliel, takes the side of the apostles in thinking that their enterprise possibly "comes from God" (Acts 5:39). Then opposition decreases for a while. It flares up again in Hellenistic synagogues when Stephen, himself a Hellenistic Jew, works "great wonders and signs among the people" (6:8–15). At the end of his discourse before members of the Sanhedrin, Stephen has recourse to the invective of the prophets (7:51). He is stoned. Following Jesus' example, he prays to the Lord that "this sin be not held against them" (7:60; cf. Lk 23:34). "That day a severe persecution began against the Church in Jerusalem" (Acts 8:1). "Saul" zealously took part in it (8:3; 9:13).

After his conversion and during all his missionary journeys, he himself—as we have already noted—experiences the opposition of his fellow countrymen, sparked by the success of his universalist preaching. This is particularly evident immediately after his arrest in Jerusalem. When he spoke "in the Hebrew language," "the assembly of people" (21:36) first heard him calmly (22:2), but from the moment he mentions his being sent "to the nations," they get terribly agitated and demand his death (22:21–22).

Acts ends on a surprising, but all the more significant, note. Shortly after his arrival in Rome, Paul "called together the local leaders of the Jews" (28:17), a unique gesture. He wants "to convince them about Jesus both from the Law of Moses and the prophets" (28:23). What he wished to obtain was not individual adherents, but a collective decision involving the whole Jewish community. After his unsuccessful attempt, he repeats the very harsh words of Isaiah concerning the hardness of "this people" (28:25–27; Is 6:9–10), and announces instead the docile acceptance that the nations will give to the salvation offered by God (28:28). In this ending, which gives rise to interminable discussion, Luke apparently wishes to accept the undeniable fact that, in the end, the Jewish people collectively did not accept the Gospel of Christ.

At the same time, Luke wishes to reply to an objection that could be made against the Christian faith, by showing that this situation had already been foreseen in the Scriptures.

Conclusion

In Luke's oeuvre, there is no doubt that there is a profound respect for the Jewish reality insofar as it has a primary role in the divine plan of salvation. Nevertheless, in the course of the narrative tensions become obvious. Luke tones down the polemics encountered in the other Synoptics. But he is unable, it seems—and does not wish—to hide the fact that Jesus suffered fierce opposition from the leaders of his people and that, as a result, the apostolic preaching finds itself in an analogous situation. If a sober recounting of this undeniable Jewish opposition amounts to anti-Judaism, then Luke could be accused of it. But it is obvious that this way of looking at it is to be rejected. Anti-Judaism consists rather of cursing and hating the persecutors, and their people as a whole. The Gospel message, on the contrary, invites Christians to bless those who curse them, to do good to those who hate them, and to pray for those who persecute them (Lk 6:27–28), following the example of Jesus (23:34) and of the first Christian martyr (Acts 7:60). This is one of the basic lessons of Luke's work. It is regrettable that in the course of the centuries following, it has not been more faithfully followed.

4. The Gospel according to John

76. About the Jews, the Fourth Gospel has a very positive statement, made by Jesus himself in the dialogue with

the Samaritan woman: "Salvation comes from the Jews" (Jn 4:22).[325] Elsewhere, to the statement of the high priest Caiaphas who said that it was "advantageous" "to have one man die for the people," the evangelist sees a meaning in the word inspired by God and emphasizes that "Jesus was about to die for the nation," adding "not for the nation only, but to gather into one the dispersed children of God" (Jn 11:49–52). The evangelist betrays a vast knowledge of Judaism, its feasts, its Scriptures. The value of the Jewish patrimony is clearly acknowledged: Abraham saw Jesus' day and was glad (8:56); the Law is a gift given through Moses as intermediary (1:17); "the Scripture cannot be annulled" (10:35); Jesus is the one "about whom Moses in the Law and also the prophets wrote" (1:45); he is "a Jew" (4:9) and "King of Israel" (1:49) or "King of the Jews" (19:19– 22). There is no serious reason to doubt that the evangelist was Jewish and that the basic context for the composition of the Gospel was relations with the Jews.

The word "Jews" is found seventy-one times in the Fourth Gospel, usually in the plural, three times in the singular (3:25; 4:9; 18:35). It is applied especially to "Jesus" (4:9). The name "Israelite" only appears once; it is a title of honor (1:47). A certain number of Jews are well disposed to Jesus. One such is Nicodemus, a "leader of the Jews" (3:1), who saw Jesus as a teacher come from God (3:2), defends him before his Pharisee colleagues (7:50–51) and, after his death on the cross, takes charge of his burial (19:39). At the end, "many of the leaders" believed in Jesus, but lacked courage to declare them-

---

325. See above II, B, 3(b), n. 32.

selves as his disciples (12:42). The evangelist frequently reports that "many" people came to believe in Jesus.[326] The context shows that it is the Jews, except in 4:39, 41; the evangelist is sometimes precise, though rarely sufficiently so (8:31; 11:45; 12:11).

Nonetheless, "the Jews" are often hostile to Jesus. Their opposition begins with the curing of the paralytic on the sabbath day (5:16). It intensifies when Jesus makes himself "equal to God"; they try from then on to have him put to death (5:18). Later, like the high priest during the trial of Jesus in Mt 26:65 and Mk 14:64, they accuse him of "blasphemy" and try to punish him accordingly by stoning (10:31–33). It has been noted with good reason that much of the Fourth Gospel anticipates the trial of Jesus and gives him the opportunity to defend himself and accuse his accusers. These are often called "the Jews" without further precision, with the result that an unfavorable judgment is associated with that name. But there is no question here of anti-Jewish sentiment, since—as we have already noted—the Gospel recognizes that "salvation comes from the Jews" (4:22). This manner of speaking only reflects the clear separation that existed between the Christian and Jewish communities.

A more serious accusation made by Jesus against "the Jews" is that of having the devil for a father (8:44); it should be noted that this accusation is not made against the Jews insofar as they are Jews, but, on the contrary, insofar as they are not true Jews, since they entertain murderous intentions

---

326. Jn 2:23; 4:39, 41; 7:31; 8:30–31; 10:42; 11:45; 12:11, 42.

(8:37), inspired by the devil, who is "a murderer from the beginning" (8:44). The only concern here is a small number of Jesus' contemporaries, paradoxically, of "Jews who had believed in him" (8:31). By accusing them openly, the Fourth Gospel puts other Jews on guard against the temptation to similar murderous thoughts.

77. By translating "the Jews" as "the Judeans," an attempt has been made to eliminate the tensions that the Fourth Gospel can provoke between Christians and Jews. The contrast then would not be between the Jews and Jesus' disciples, but between the inhabitants of Judea, presented as hostile to Jesus, and those of Galilee, presented as flocking to their prophet. Contempt by Judeans for Galileans is certainly expressed in the Gospel (7:52), but the evangelist did not draw the lines of demarcation between faith and refusal to believe along geographical lines; he distinguishes Galilean Jews who reject Jesus' teaching as *hoi Ioudaioi* (6:41, 52).

Another interpretation of "the Jews" identifies them with "the world" based on affirmations which express a comparison (8:23) or parallelism between them.[327] But the world of sinners, by all accounts, extends beyond Jews who are hostile to Jesus.

It has also been noted that in many Gospel passages "the Jews" referred to are the Jewish authorities (chief priests, members of the Sanhedrin) or sometimes the Pharisees. A comparison between 18:3 and 18:12 points in this direction. In the passion narrative, John frequently mentions "the Jews" where the Synoptics speak of Jewish authorities. But this

---

327. Jn 1:10, 11; 15:18, 25.

observation holds good only for a certain restricted number of passages, and such precision cannot be introduced into a translation of the Gospel without being unfaithful to the text. These are echoes of opposition to Christian communities, not only on the part of the Jewish authorities, but from the vast majority of Jews, in solidarity with their leaders (cf. Acts 28:22). Historically, it can be said that only a minority of Jews contemporaneous with Jesus were hostile to him, that a smaller number were responsible for handing him over to the Roman authorities, and that fewer still wanted him killed, undoubtedly for religious reasons that seemed important to them.[328] But these succeeded in provoking a general demonstration in favor of Barabbas and against Jesus,[329] which permitted the evangelist to use a general expression, anticipating a later evolution.

At times in the Gospel the separation of Jesus' disciples from "the Jews" is evident in the expulsion from the synagogue imposed on Jews who believed in Jesus.[330] It is possible that the Jews in the Johannine communities experienced this treatment, since they would be considered unfaithful to Jewish monotheistic faith (which, in fact, was not at all the case, since Jesus said: "I and the Father *are one":* 10:30). The result was that it became almost standard to use "the Jews" to designate those who kept this name for themselves alone, in their opposition to the Christian faith.

78. *Conclusion.* The ministry of Jesus stirred up mounting opposition on the part of the Jewish authorities, who finally

---

328. Jn 5:18; 10:33; 19:7.
329. Jn 18:38–40; 19:14–15.
330. Jn 9:22; 12:42; 16:2.

decided to hand Jesus over to the Roman authorities to have him put to death. But he arose alive to give true life to all who believe in him. The Fourth Gospel recalls these events, and re-evaluates them in the light of the experience of the Johannine communities that had encountered opposition from the Jewish communities.

The actions and words of Jesus show that he had a very close filial relationship with God that was unique of its kind. The apostolic catechesis progressively deepened its understanding of this relationship. In the Johannine communities, there was an insistence on the close relationship between Son and Father and on the divinity of Jesus, who is "the Christ, the Son of God" (20:31) in a transcendent sense. This teaching provoked opposition from the synagogue leaders, followed by the whole Jewish community. Christians were expelled from the synagogues (16:2) and were exposed, at the same time, to harassment by the Roman authorities, since they no longer enjoyed the franchise granted to Jews.

The polemic escalated on both sides. The Jews accused Jesus of being a sinner (9:24), a blasphemer (10:33) and of having a devil.[331] Those who believed in him were considered ignorant or accursed (7:49). On the Christian side, Jews were accused of disobedience to God's word (5:38), resisting his love (5:42), and pursuing vainglory (5:44).

Christians, no longer able to participate in Jewish cultic life, became more aware of the plenitude they had received from the Word made flesh (1:16). The risen Christ is the source of living water (7:37–38), light of the world (8:12),

---

331. Jn 7:20; 8:48, 51; 10:20.

bread of life (6:35), and new Temple (2:19– 22). Having loved his own to the end (13:1), he gave them his new commandment of love (13:34). Everything must be done to stir up faith in him, and, through faith, life (20:31). In the Gospel, polemics are secondary. What is of the greatest importance is the revelation of the "gift of God" (4:10; 3:16), which is offered to all in Jesus Christ, especially to those "who have pierced him" (19:37).

5. Conclusion

The Gospels reveal that the fulfillment of God's plan necessarily brought with it a confrontation with evil, which must be eradicated from the human heart. This confrontation puts Jesus at odds with the leaders of his people, just like the ancient prophets. Already in the Old Testament, the people of God were seen under two antithetical aspects: on the one hand, as a people called to be perfectly united to God; and on the other, as a sinful people. These two aspects could not fail to manifest themselves during Jesus' ministry. During the passion, the negative aspect seemed to prevail, even among the Twelve. But the resurrection showed that, in reality, the love of God was victorious and obtained for all the pardon of sin and a new life.

C. The Jews in the Pauline Letters and Other New Testament Writings

79. The Pauline Letters will be considered in accordance with the most commonly accepted groupings: first, seven letters generally recognized as authentic (Rm, 1—2 Co, Gal, Ph,

1 Th, Phm), then Ephesians and Colossians, the Pastorals (1—2 Tm, Tt). Finally, the Letter to the Hebrews, the Letters of Peter, James and Jude, and the Book of Revelation will be looked at.

1. Jews in the undisputed Pauline Letters

Personally, Paul continued to be proud of his Jewish origin (Rm 11:1). Referring to the time preceding his conversion, he says: "I advanced in Judaism beyond many among my people of the same age, for I was far more zealous for the traditions of my ancestors" (Gal 1:14). Having become an apostle of Christ, he says of his adversaries: "Are they Hebrews? So am I. Are they Israelites? So am I. Are they descendants of Abraham? So am I" (2 Co 11:22). Still, he can relativize all these advantages by saying: "These I have come to regard as loss because of Christ" (Ph 3:7).

Nonetheless, he continues to think and reason like a Jew. His thought is visibly permeated by Jewish ideas. In his writings, as was mentioned above, we find not only continual references to the Old Testament, but many traces of Jewish traditions as well. Furthermore, Paul often uses rabbinic techniques of exegesis and argumentation (cf. above n. 14).

Paul's ties to Judaism are also seen in his moral teaching. In spite of his opposition to the pretensions of those who kept the Law, he himself includes a precept of the Law, Lv 19:18 ("You shall love your neighbor as yourself") to sum up the whole of the moral life.[332] Summing up the Law in one precept is typically Jewish, as the well-known anecdote about

---

332. Gal 5:14; Rm 13:9.

Rabbi Hillel and Rabbi Shammai, Jesus' contemporaries, demonstrates.[333]

What attitude did the Apostle adopt toward the Jews? In principle, a positive one. He calls them: "My brothers, my kindred according to the flesh" (Rm 9:3). Convinced that the Gospel of Christ is "the power of God for the salvation of everyone who has faith, to the Jews first" (Rm 1:16), he desired to transmit the faith to them and spared no effort to that end. He could say: "To the Jews I became a Jew, in order to win Jews" (1 Co 9:20) and even: "To those under the Law I became as one under the Law—though I myself am not under the Law—so that I might win those under the Law" (1 Co 9:20). Likewise in his apostolate to the Gentiles, he endeavored to be indirectly useful to his fellow Jews, "in the hope of saving some of them" (Rm 11:14). For this, he relied on emulation (11:11, 14): that the sight of the marvelous spiritual enrichment that faith in Christ Jesus gave to pagan converts would stir up the desire among the Jews not to be outdone, and would lead them also to be receptive to the faith.

The resistance mounted by the majority of Jews to the Christian preaching produced in Paul's heart "great sorrow and unceasing anguish" (Rm 9:2), clear evidence of his great affection for them. He said that he himself was willing to accept on their behalf the greatest and most inconceivable sacrifice, to be branded "accursed," separated from Christ (9:3). His afflictions and suffering forced him to search for a solution: in three lengthy chapters (Rm 9—11), he goes to the heart of the problem, or rather the mystery, of Israel's place in

---

333. Cf. Babylonian Talmud, Tract Shabbat 31a.

God's plan, in the light of Christ and of the Scriptures, without giving up until he is able to conclude: "and so all Israel will be saved" (Rm 11:26). These three chapters in the Letter to the Romans constitute the most profound reflection in the whole of the New Testament on Jews who do not believe in Jesus. Paul expressed there his most mature reflections.

The solution he proposed is based on the Scriptures which, in certain places, promised salvation only to a "remnant" of Israel.[334] In this phase of salvation history then, there is only a "remnant" of Israelites who believe in Christ Jesus, but this situation is not definitive. Paul observes that, from now on, the presence of the "remnant" proves that God has not "rejected his people" (11:1). This people continues to be "holy," that is, in close relationship with God. It is holy because it comes from a holy root, the ancestors, and because their "first fruits" have been blessed (11:16). Paul does not make it clear whether by "first fruits" he means Israel's ancestors, or the "remnant" sanctified by faith and baptism. He exploits the agricultural metaphor of the tree when he speaks of branches being cut off and grafted (11:17–24). It is understood that the cut off branches are Israelites who have refused to believe in Christ Jesus and that those grafted on are Gentile Christians. To these—as we have already noted—Paul preaches humility: "It is not you that support the root, but the root that supports you" (11:18). To the branches that have been cut off, Paul opens up a positive perspective: "God has the power to graft them on again" (11:23); this would be easier than in the case

---

334. Rm 9:27–29, quoting Is 10:22–23; Hos 2:1 LXX; Rm 11:4–5 quoting 1 Kg 19:18.

of the Gentiles, since it is "their own olive tree" (11:24). In the final analysis, God's plan for Israel is entirely positive: "their stumbling means riches for the world," "how much more will their full inclusion mean?" (11:12). They are assured of a covenant of mercy by God (11:27, 31).

80. In the years preceding the writing of the Letter to the Romans, because he experienced fierce opposition from many of his "relatives according to the flesh," Paul occasionally expressed strong defensive reactions. On the opposition of the Jews, Paul wrote: "From the Jews I received forty lashes minus one" (cf. Dt 25:3). A little later he notes what he must do in the face of danger from brothers of his race as well as from Gentiles (2 Co 11:24, 26). The recalling of these sad experiences elicits no comment from Paul. He is ready to "participate in the sufferings of Christ" (Ph 3:10). But what provokes an animated reaction are the obstacles placed by Jews in the way of his apostolate to the Gentiles. This is evident in a passage in the First Letter to the Thessalonians (2:14–16). These verses are so much at variance with Paul's habitual attitude toward the Jews that attempts have been made to demonstrate that they are not from Paul, or to play down their vehemence. But the unanimous testimony of manuscripts renders their exclusion impossible, and the tenor of the whole does not permit restriction to the inhabitants of Judea, as has been suggested. The final verse is pungent: "God's wrath has overtaken them at last" (1 Th 2:16). One is reminded of Jeremiah's predictions[335] and of a phrase in 2 Ch

---

335. Jer 7:16, 20; 11:11, 14; 15:1.

36:16: "The wrath of the Lord against his people became so great that there was no remedy." These predicted the national catastrophe of 587 B.C.: the siege and capture of Jerusalem, the burning of the Temple, the deportation. Paul apparently foresees a catastrophe of similar proportions. It is worth noting, though, that the events of 587 were not the end. The Lord then had pity on his people. It follows that the terrible prediction of Paul—one which unfortunately came to pass—did not exclude a subsequent reconciliation.

In 1 Th 2:14–16, in the context of sufferings inflicted on the Thessalonian Christians by their compatriots, Paul recalls that the churches in Judea had suffered the same fate at the hands of the Jews, and accuses them of a series of crimes: they "killed the Lord Jesus and the prophets and also drove us out"; then in the present tense: "they displease God and are hostile to all men in their effort to keep us from speaking to the Gentiles so that they may be saved." It is clear that the last is more important to Paul than the two preceding negative appraisals. Because the Jews are an obstacle to the Christian preaching addressed to the Gentiles, they "oppose all men"[336] and "they displease God." In opposing the Christian preaching, the Jews of Paul's time show themselves in solidarity with the ancestors who killed the prophets, and with their own brothers who demanded that Jesus be condemned to death.

---

336. Their rejection of idolatry and their contempt for paganism gave rise to strong animosity toward the Jews, accused of being a people apart (Est 3:8), "in conflict in everything with all people" (Est 3:13e LXX), and of nourishing a "hatred of enemies toward all other (people)" (Tacitus, *History,* 5:5). Paul's viewpoint is quite different.

The formulae used by Paul seem to suggest that the death of Jesus is to be attributed to all Jews indiscriminately without distinction: anti-Jewish interpreters understand them in this sense. Put in context, however, they refer only to Jews who were opposed to preaching to the pagans and therefore opposed their salvation. When the opposition ceases, the accusation does as well.

Another polemical passage is found in Ph 3:2–3: "Beware of the dogs, beware of the evil workers, beware of those who mutilate the flesh *(katatomē)!* For it is we who are the circumcision *(peritomē)."* Whom has the Apostle in mind here? Since the reference is not explicit enough, it does not allow us any certainty, but the interpretation that Jews are envisaged can at least be excluded. According to a current opinion, Paul would have in mind judaizing Christians, who wished to impose circumcision on Christians from the "nations." Paul aggressively applies to them a term of contempt, "dogs," a metaphor for the ritual impurity that the Jews sometimes attributed to the Gentiles (Mt 15:26). He downgrades circumcision of the flesh by ironically calling it "mutilation" (cf. Gal 5:12), and opposes to it a spiritual circumcision, similar to Deuteronomy's circumcision of the heart.[337] The context, in this case, would have been the controversy about Jewish observances within the Christian churches, as in the Letter to the Galatians. It would probably be better to see a reference, as in Rv 22:15, to the pagan context in which the Philippians lived, and to assume that Paul is referring here to pagan customs:

---

337. Dt 10:16; cf. Jer 4:4; Rm 2:29.

sexual perversions, immoral acts, cultic mutilations associated with orgiastic cults.[338]

81. On the matter of Abraham's descendants, Paul makes a distinction—as we have already indicated—between the "children of the promise like Isaac," who are also children "according to the Spirit," and children "according to the flesh."[339] It is not enough to be "children of the flesh" in order to be "children of God" (Rm 9:8), for the essential condition is commitment to him whom "God has sent...so that we might receive the adoption of sons" (Gal 4:4–5).

In another context, the Apostle omits this distinction, and speaks of the Jews in general. He declares that they have the privilege of being the depositories of divine revelation (Rm 3:1–2). Nevertheless, this privilege has not exempted them from sin's dominion over them (3:9–19); hence it is still necessary to gain justification by faith in Christ rather than by the observance of the Law (3:20–22).

When he considers the situation of Jews who have not followed Christ, Paul insists on affirming his profound esteem for them by enumerating the marvelous gifts which they have received from God: "They are Israelites, and to them belong the adoption, the glory, the covenants, the giving of the Law, the worship and the promises; to them belong the patriarchs, and from them, according to the flesh, comes the Messiah,

---

338. Cf. 1 Co 6:9–11; Ep 4:17–19. In Dt 23:19, "dog" designates a prostitute; in Greece, the dog was a symbol of lewdness. For ritual mutilations, cf. Lv 21:5; 1 Kg 18:28; Is 15:2; Hos 7:14.

339. Gal 4:28–29; Rm 9:8.

who is over all, God blessed forever. Amen" (Rm 9:4–5).[340] Despite the absence of verbs, it can scarcely be doubted that Paul wishes to speak of these gifts as still actually possessed (cf. 11:29), even if, from his viewpoint, possession of them is not sufficient, for they refuse God's most important gift, his Son, although physically he is one with them. Paul attests that "they are zealous for God," adding: "but it is not enlightened. For being ignorant of the righteousness that comes from God, and seeking to establish their own, they have not submitted to God's righteousness" (10:2–3). Nevertheless, God does not abandon them. His plan is to show them mercy. "The hardening" which affects "a part of" Israel is only provisional and has its usefulness for the time being (11:25); it will be followed by salvation (11:26). Paul sums up the situation in an antithetical phrase, followed by a positive affirmation:

"As regards the Gospel they are enemies of God for your sake; as regards election they are beloved, for the sake of their ancestors; for the gifts and the calling of God are irrevocable" (11:28–29).

Paul views the situation realistically. Between Christ's disciples and the Jews who do not believe in him, the relation is one of opposition. These Jews call the Christian faith into question; they do not accept that Jesus is their Messiah *(Christ)* and the Son of God. Christians cannot but contest the

---

340. In Greek, for "to them belong" there is a simple genitive twice, which expresses possession (literally: "of whom [are]"); for "from them comes" there is a genitive introduced by the preposition *ex* which expresses origin.

position of these Jews. But at a level deeper than opposition there exists from now on a loving relationship that is definitive; the other is only temporary.

2. Jews in the other Letters

82. The Letter to the *Colossians* contains the word "Jew" only once, in a sentence that says in the new man "there is no longer Greek and Jew," adding as well a parallel expression: "circumcised and uncircumcised"; there is only Christ "who is all and in all" (Col 3:11). This phrase, which recalls the teaching of Gal 3:28 and Rm 10:12, denies any importance to being a Jew from the point of view of a relationship with Christ. It passes no judgment on Jews, any more than it does on Greeks.

The value of circumcision before the coming of Christ is indirectly affirmed, when the author recalls for the Colossians that formerly they were "dead in trespasses and the uncircumcision of [their] flesh" (2:13). But the value of Jewish circumcision is eclipsed by "circumcision in Christ," "a circumcision not made with hands, by putting off the body of the flesh" (2:11); there is here an allusion to Christians' participation in Christ's death through baptism (cf. Rm 6:3–6). The result is that Jews who do not believe in Christ are in an unsatisfactory situation from a religious point of view, but this is not expressed.

The Letter to the *Ephesians* does not use the word "Jew" even once. It mentions only once "uncircumcision" and "circumcision," in a phrase alluding to the contempt that Jews have for pagans. The latter were "called 'the uncircumcision' by those who are called 'the circumcision'" (2:11). Elsewhere, in conformity with the teaching of the Letters to the Galatians and Romans, the author, speaking in the name of Jewish-Christians, describes in negative terms the situation of Jews before their conversion: they were among the "sons of disobedience" together with the pagans (2:2–3), and their conduct served "the passions of [their] flesh"; they were then "by nature children of wrath, like everyone else" (2:3). However, another passage in the Letter indirectly gives a different image of the situation of the Jews, this time a positive image, by describing the sad lot of non-Jews who were "without Christ, excluded from citizenship in Israel and foreigners to the covenants of the promise, without hope and without God in the world" (2:12). The privileges of the Jews are here recalled and greatly appreciated.

The principal theme of the Letter is precisely an enthusiastic affirmation that those privileges, brought to their culmination by Christ's coming, are henceforth accessible to the Gentiles, who "have become fellow heirs, members of the same body, and sharers in the promise in Christ Jesus" (3:6). The crucifixion of Christ is understood as an event that has destroyed the wall of separation erected by the Law between Jews and Gentiles, and so has demolished the hatred between them (2:14). The perspective is one of perfectly harmonious relations. Christ is the peace between both, in such a way as to create from the two a unique new man, and to reconcile both with God in one body (2:15–16). The refusal of the Christian faith given by the majority of Jews is not mentioned. The atmosphere remains irenic.

Concerned with the internal organization of the Christian communities, the *Pastoral Letters* never speak of the Jews.

There is a single allusion to "those of the circumcision" (Ti 1:10), but this refers to Jewish-Christians belonging to the community. They are criticized for being, more so than other members of the community, "rebellious people, idle talkers and deceivers." Besides, the putting on guard against "endless genealogies" found in 1 Ti 1:10 and Ti 3:9, probably refers to Jewish speculations about Old Testament personages, "Jewish myths" (Ti 1:4).

Neither does the Letter to the *Hebrews* mention "the Jews" or even "the Hebrews"! It does mention once "the sons of Israel," in reference to the Exodus (Heb 11:22), and twice "the people of God."[341] It speaks of Jewish priests when it recalls "those who officiate in the tent" (13:10), pointing out the distance that separates them from the Christian cult. On the positive side, it recalls Jesus' connection with "the descendants of Abraham" (2:16) and the tribe of Judah (7:14). The author points out the deficiencies of Old Testament institutions, especially the sacrificial cult, but always basing himself on the Old Testament itself, whose value as divine revelation he always fully recognizes. With regard to the Israelites of the past, the author's appreciation is not one-sided, but corresponds faithfully to that of the Old Testament itself: that is, on the one hand, by quoting and commenting on Ps 95:7–11, he recalls the lack of faith of the generation of the Exodus,[342] but on the other hand, he paints a magnificent fresco of examples of faith given throughout the ages by Abraham and his descendants (11:8–38). Speaking of Christ's

---

341. Heb 4:9; 11:25; cf. 10:30 "his people."
342. Nm 14:1– 35; Heb 3:7—4:11.

passion, the Letter to the Hebrews makes no mention of the responsibility of the Jewish authorities, but simply says that Jesus endured strong opposition "on the part of sinners."[343]

The same holds for the *First Letter of Peter,* which evokes Christ's passion by saying that "the Lord" was "rejected *by men*" (1 Pt 2:4) without further precision. The letter confers on Christians the glorious titles of the Israelite people,[344] but without any polemical intent. It never mentions the Jews. The same is true for the Letter of James, the Second Letter of Peter and the Letter of Jude. These letters are steeped in Jewish teaching, but do not touch on the relationship between the Christian Church and contemporary Jews.

3. Jews in the Book of Revelation

83. A very favorable attitude toward the Jews is evident throughout the book, but especially in the mention of 144,000 "servants of our God" marked "on their foreheads" with the "sign of the living God" (Rv 7:2–4) coming from all the tribes of Israel which are enumerated one by one (a unique case in the New Testament: Rv 7:5–8). Revelation reaches its high point in its description of "the new Jerusalem" (Rv 21:2) with its "twelve gates" on which the names are inscribed "which are those of the twelve tribes of Israel" (21:12), in parallel to "the names of the twelve apostles of the Lamb," inscribed on the twelve foundations of the city (21:14).

Regarding the "so-called Jews" mentioned in two parallel passages (2:9 and 3:9), the author rejects their pretensions and

---

343. Heb 12:3; cf. Lk 24:7.
344. 1 Pt 2:9; Ex 19:6; Is 43:21.

calls them a "synagogue of Satan." In 2:9, these "so–called Jews" are accused of defaming the Christian community of Smyrna. In 3:9, Christ announces that they will be compelled to pay homage to the Christians of Philadelphia. These passages suggest that Christians are denying the title of Jew to the Israelites who defame them, and range themselves on the side of Satan, "the accuser of our brothers" (Rv 12:10). There is then a positive appreciation of "Jew" as a title of honor, an honor that is denied to a synagogue which is actively hostile to Christians.

IV.

Conclusions

A. General Conclusion

84. At the end of this exposition, necessarily all too brief, the main conclusion to be drawn is that the Jewish people and their Sacred Scriptures occupy a very important place in the Christian Bible. Indeed, the Jewish Sacred Scriptures constitute an essential part of the Christian Bible and are present, in a variety of ways, in the other part of the Christian Bible as well. Without the Old Testament, the New Testament would be an incomprehensible book, a plant deprived of its roots and destined to dry up and wither.

The New Testament recognizes the divine authority of the Jewish Scriptures and supports itself on this authority. When the New Testament speaks of the "Scriptures" and refers to "that which is written," it is to the Jewish Scriptures that it refers. It affirms that these Scriptures must of necessity be fulfilled, since they define God's plan which cannot fail to be realized, notwithstanding the obstacles encountered and the human resistance opposing it. To that the New Testament adds that these Scriptures are indeed fulfilled in the life of

Jesus, his passion and resurrection, as well as in the foundation of the Church that is open to all the nations. All of these bind Christians and Jews closely together, for the foremost aspect of scriptural fulfillment is that of accord and continuity. This is fundamental. Inevitably, fulfillment brings discontinuity on certain points, because without it there can be no progress. This discontinuity is a source of disagreements between Christians and Jews; no purpose is served by hiding the fact. But it was wrong, in times past, to unilaterally insist on it to the extent of taking no account of the fundamental continuity.

This continuity has deep roots and manifests itself at many levels. That is why in Christianity the link between Scripture and Tradition is similar to that in Judaism. Jewish methods of exegesis are frequently employed in the New Testament. The Christian canon of the Old Testament owes its formation to the first century Jewish Scriptures. To properly interpret the New Testament, knowledge of the Judaism of this period is often necessary.

85. But it is especially seen in studying the great themes of the Old Testament and their continuation in the New, which accounts for the impressive symbiosis that unites the two parts of the Christian Bible and, at the same time, the vigorous spiritual ties that unite the Church of Christ to the Jewish people. In both Testaments, it is the same God who enters into relationship with human beings and invites them to live in communion with him, the one God and the source of unity; God the Creator continues to provide for the needs of his creatures, in particular those who are intelligent and free, and

who are called to recognize the truth and to love; God especially is the Liberator and Savior of human beings, because, although created in his image, they have fallen through sin into a pitiful slavery.

Since it is a project for interpersonal relationships, God's plan is realized in history. It is impossible to discover what that plan is by philosophical speculation on the human being in general. God reveals this plan by unforeseeable initiatives, in particular, by the call addressed to an individual chosen from all the rest of humanity, Abraham (Gn 12:1–3), and by guiding the destiny of this person and his posterity, the people of Israel (Ex 3:10). A central Old Testament theme (Dt 7:6–8), Israel's election, continues to be of fundamental importance in the New Testament. Far from calling it into question, the birth of Jesus confirms it in the most spectacular manner. Jesus is "son of David, son of Abraham" (Mt 1:1). He comes "to save his people from their sins" (1:21). He is the Messiah promised to Israel (Jn 1:41, 45); he is "the Word" *(Logos)* come "to his own" (Jn 1:11–14). The salvation he brings through his paschal mystery is offered first of all to the Israelites.[345] As foreseen by the Old Testament, this salvation has universal repercussions as well.[346] It is also offered to the Gentiles. Moreover, it is accepted by many of them, to the extent that they have become the great majority of Christ's disciples. But Christians from the nations profit from salvation only by being introduced, by their faith in Israel's

---

345. Acts 3:26; Rm 1:16.
346. Ps 98:2–4; Is 49:6.

Messiah, into the posterity of Abraham (Gal 3:7, 29). Many Christians from the "nations" are not aware that they are by nature "wild olives" and that their faith in Christ has grafted them onto the olive tree chosen by God (Rm 11:17–18).

Israel's election is made concrete and specific in the Sinai covenant and by the institutions based on it, especially the Law and the Temple. The New Testament is in continuity with this covenant and its institutions. The new covenant foretold by Jeremiah and established in the blood of Jesus has come through the covenant between God and Israel, surpassing the Sinai covenant by a new gift of the Lord that completes and carries forward the original gift. Likewise, "the law of the Spirit of life in Christ Jesus" (Rm 8:2), which gives an interior dynamism, remedies the weakness (8:3) of the Sinai Law and renders believers capable of living a disinterested love that is the "fulfillment of the Law" (Rm 13:10). As regards the earthly Temple, the New Testament—borrowing terms prepared by the Old Testament—relativizes the adequacy of a material edifice as a dwelling place of God (Acts 7:48), and points to a relationship with God where the emphasis is on interiority. In this point, as in many others, it is obvious that the continuity is based on the prophetic movement of the Old Testament.

In the past, the break between the Jewish people and the Church of Christ Jesus could sometimes, in certain times and places, give the impression of being complete. In the light of the Scriptures, this should never have occurred. For a complete break between Church and Synagogue contradicts Sacred Scripture.

B. Pastoral Orientations

86. The Second Vatican Council, in its recommendation that there be "understanding and mutual esteem" between Christians and Jews, declared that these will be "born especially from biblical and theological study, as well as from fraternal dialogue."[347] The present document has been composed in this spirit; it hopes to make a positive contribution to it, and encourages in the Church of Christ the love toward Jews that Pope Paul VI emphasized on the day of the promulgation of the conciliar document *Nostra Aetate*.[348]

With this text, Vatican II laid the foundations for a new understanding of our relations with Jews when it said that "according to the Apostle [Paul], the Jews, because of their ancestors, still remain very dear to God, whose gifts and calling are irrevocable (Rm 11:29)."[349]

Through his teaching, John Paul II has, on many occasions, taken the initiative in developing this Declaration. During a visit to the synagogue of Mainz (1980) he said: "The encounter between the people of God of the Old Covenant, which has never been abrogated by God (cf. Rm 11:29), and that of the New Covenant is also an *internal* dialogue in our Church, similar to that between the first and second part of its

---

347. Declaration "Nostra Aetate" on relations of the Church with non-Christian religions, n. 4.

348. Paul VI, homily of October 28, 1965: *"ut erga eos reverentia et amor adhibeatur spesque in iis collocetur"* ("that there be respect and love toward them and that hope is placed in them").

349. *ASS* 58 (1966) 740.

Bible."[350] Later, addressing the Jewish communities of Italy during a visit to the synagogue of Rome (1986), he declared: "The Church of Christ discovers its 'links' with Judaism 'by pondering its own mystery' (cf. *Nostra Aetate*). The Jewish religion is not 'extrinsic' to us, but in a certain manner, it is 'intrinsic' to our religion. We have therefore a relationship with it which we do not have with any other religion. You are our favored brothers and, in a certain sense, one can say our elder brothers."[351] Finally, in the course of a meeting on the roots of anti-Jewish feeling among Christians (1997), he said: "This people has been called and led by God, Creator of heaven and earth. Their existence then is not a mere natural or cultural happening.... It is a supernatural one. This people continues in spite of everything to be the people of the covenant and, despite human infidelity, the Lord is faithful to his covenant."[352] This teaching was given the stamp of approval by John Paul II's visit to Israel, in the course of which he addressed Israel's Chief Rabbis in these terms: "We [Jews and Christians] must work together to build a future in which there will be no more anti-Jewish feeling among Christians, or any anti-Christian feeling among Jews. We have many things in common. We can do much for the sake of peace, for a more human and more fraternal world."[353]

On the part of Christians, the main condition for progress along these lines lies in avoiding a one-sided reading of bibli-

---

350. *Documentation Catholique* 77 (1980) 1148.

351. *Documentation Catholique* 83 (1986) 437.

352. *Documentation Catholique* 94 (1997) 1003.

353. *Documentation Catholique* 97 (2000) 372.

cal texts, both from the Old Testament and the New Testament, and making instead a better effort to appreciate the whole dynamism that animates them, which is precisely a dynamism of love. In the Old Testament, the plan of God is a union of love with his people, a paternal love, a spousal love and, notwithstanding Israel's infidelities, God will never renounce it, but affirms it in perpetuity (Is 54:8; Jer 31:3). In the New Testament, God's love overcomes the worst obstacles; even if they do not believe in his Son whom he sent as their Messiah Savior, Israelites are still "loved" (Rm 11:29). Whoever wishes to be united to God must also love them.

87. The partial reading of texts frequently gives rise to difficulties affecting relations with the Jews. The Old Testament, as we have seen, is not sparing in its reproaches against Israelites, or even in its condemnations. It is very demanding toward them. Rather than casting stones at the Jews, it is better to see them as illustrating the saying of the Lord Jesus: "To whom much is given, from him much is expected" (Lk 12:48), and this saying applies to us Christians as well. Certain biblical narratives present aspects of disloyalty or cruelty which today would be morally inadmissible, but they must be understood in their historical and literary contexts. The slow historical progress of revelation must be recognized: the divine pedagogy has taken a group of people where it found them and led them patiently in the direction of an ideal union with God and toward a moral integrity which our modern society is still far from attaining. This education must avoid two opposite dangers, on the one hand, of attributing to ancient prescriptions an ongoing validity for Christians (for example, refusing blood transfusions on biblical grounds) and,

on the other hand, of rejecting the whole Bible on the pretext of its cruelties. As regards ritual precepts, such as the rules for pure and impure, one has to be conscious of their symbolic and anthropological import, and be aware of their sociological and religious functions.

In the New Testament, the reproaches addressed to Jews are not as frequent or as virulent as the accusations against Jews in the Law and the Prophets. Therefore, they no longer serve as a basis for anti-Jewish sentiment. To use them for this purpose is contrary to the whole tenor of the New Testament. Real anti-Jewish feeling, that is, an attitude of contempt, hostility and persecution of the Jews as Jews, is not found in any New Testament text and is incompatible with its teaching. What is found are reproaches addressed to certain categories of Jews for religious reasons, as well as polemical texts to defend the Christian apostolate against Jews who oppose it.

But it must be admitted that many of these passages are capable of providing a pretext for anti-Jewish sentiment and have in fact been used in this way. To avoid mistakes of this kind, it must be kept in mind that the New Testament polemical texts, even those expressed in general terms, have to do with concrete historical contexts and are never meant to be applied to Jews of all times and places merely because they are Jews. The tendency to speak in general terms, to accentuate the adversaries' negative side, and to pass over the positive in silence; failure to consider their motivations and their ultimate good faith—these are characteristics of all polemical language throughout antiquity, and are no less evident in Judaism and primitive Christianity against all kinds of dissidents.

The fact that the New Testament is essentially a proclamation of the fulfillment of God's plan in Jesus Christ puts it in serious disagreement with the vast majority of the Jewish people who do not accept this fulfillment. The New Testament then expresses at one and the same time its attachment to Old Testament revelation and its disagreement with the Synagogue. This discord is not to be taken as "anti-Jewish sentiment," for it is disagreement at the level of faith, the source of religious controversy between two human groups that take their point of departure from the same Old Testament faith basis, but are in disagreement on how to conceive the final development of that faith. Although profound, such disagreement in no way implies reciprocal hostility. The example of Paul in Rm 9—11 shows that, on the contrary, an attitude of respect, esteem and love for the Jewish people is the only truly Christian attitude in a situation which is mysteriously part of the beneficent and positive plan of God. Dialogue is possible, since Jews and Christians share a rich common patrimony that unites them. It is greatly to be desired that prejudice and misunderstanding be gradually eliminated on both sides, in favor of a better understanding of the patrimony they share and to strengthen the links that bind them.

Related titles from Pauline Books & Media

By the Pontifical Biblical Commission:

The Historicity of the Gospels
16 pp., # 3344–4

The Interpretation of the Bible in the Church
135 pp., # 3670–2

By the Pontifical Commission for Religious Relations with the Jews:

We Remember: A Reflection on the Shoah
24pp., # 8296–8

By Luigi Accattoli:

When a Pope Asks Forgiveness
The Mea Culpa's of John Paul II
264 pp., # 8295–X

Order Today!
www.pauline.org
1-800-876-4463

BOOKS & MEDIA
BOSTON

BOOKS & MEDIA

The Daughters of St. Paul operate book and media centers at the following addresses. Visit, call or write the one nearest you today, or find us on the World Wide Web, www.pauline.org

California
3908 Sepulveda Blvd, Culver City,
  CA 90230   310-397-8676
5945 Balboa Avenue, San Diego,
  CA 92111   858-565-9181
46 Geary Street, San Francisco,
  CA 94108   415-781-5180

Florida
145 S.W. 107th Avenue, Miami,
  FL 33174   305-559-6715

Hawaii
1143 Bishop Street, Honolulu,
  HI 96813   808-521-2731
Neighbor Islands call: 800-259-8463

Illinois
172 North Michigan Avenue,
  Chicago, IL 60601
  312-346-4228

Louisiana
4403 Veterans Memorial Blvd,
  Metairie, LA 70006
  504-887-7631

Massachusetts
885 Providence Hwy, Dedham,
  MA 02026   781-326-5385

Missouri
9804 Watson Road, St. Louis,
  MO 63126   314-965-3512

New Jersey
561 U.S. Route 1, Wick Plaza,
  Edison, NJ 08817   732-572-1200

New York
150 East 52nd Street, New York,
  NY 10022   212-754-1110
78 Fort Place, Staten Island, NY
  10301   718-447-5071

Pennsylvania
9171-A Roosevelt Blvd, Philadelphia,
  PA 19114   215-676-9494

South Carolina
243 King Street, Charleston, SC
  29401   843-577-0175

Tennessee
4811 Poplar Avenue, Memphis,
  TN 38117   901-761-2987

Texas
114 Main Plaza, San Antonio, TX
  78205   210-224-8101

Virginia
1025 King Street, Alexandria, VA
  22314   703-549-3806

Canada
3022 Dufferin Street, Toronto, Ontario,
  Canada M6B 3T5   416-781-9131
1155 Yonge Street, Toronto, Ontario,
  Canada M4T 1W2   416-934-3440

¡También somos su fuente para libros, videos y música en español!